HOW IT ALL FITS TOGETHER

**KNOWING WISDOM
IN PROVERBS**

BILL SMITH

How It All Fits Together
Knowing the Wisdom of Proverbs

Athanasius Press
715 Cypress Street
West Monroe, Louisiana, 71291
athanasiuspress.org | (318) 323-3061

Cover design and typesetting: Rachel Rosales

ISBN: 978-1-957726-07-6

Printed in the United States of America.

To my children,
Nathan, Joshua, David, Joanna,
Caleb, and Sophia:

May you continue to pursue wisdom
for the rest of your days.

Contents

Introduction

When I was a young parent, I was terrified of the prospect of training little souls that would one day become big souls. I did not have what would be called an optimal upbringing. It was not terrible, but it was not great either. Consequently, I searched for mentors, whether in books or people, to help me in the rearing of my children.

My wife, Susan, and I devoured books and listened to teaching. One of those books was *Shepherding a Child's Heart* by Tedd Tripp. Whatever you think of Tripp or the book itself, he gave me one parental discipline for which I am forever grateful: read Proverbs to your children every day. Every morning for over two decades, we read sections of chapters. (Well, I must confess: there were some missed days in there, but we regularly kept up.) When we finished reading through Proverbs, I would start again. The book of Proverbs was the principal catechism for my children. My sixth child is named Sophia because of our consistent

Proverbs reading. When Susan was pregnant with her, and we knew the child was, indeed, a girl, our other five children heard so often, "Say to wisdom, 'You are my sister…'" (Prov 7:4), to the extent that "wisdom" was the obvious choice for our child's name. (No one liked the Hebrew name *Chokhmah,* so we went with the Greek version.) As we read through the book over and over again, I realized why this was such a good idea: God designed it as a catechism in wisdom for young men especially, but also for young women. With four sons and two daughters, I had to apply the book's wisdom to sons and daughters.

For years, I read Proverbs to my family, but I never dared preach through it. I did not consider the book unpreachable but *too preachable.* I could spend the rest of my life tracing the themes of Proverbs and unearthing the wise implications of each and every statement. Besides that, the detailed structure of the book is practically unknowable in detail, though many have tried. (I say something about this in Chapter Three.) A sermon on every proverb would take years to preach through the entire book. Nevertheless, in 2021, I began teaching the book of Proverbs. One can teach straight through the book or trace the themes in Proverbs, both with great benefit. I chose to go the thematic route. This book and the books to follow (Lord willing) are the fruit of that series of sermons.

In this volume, I hope to acquaint the reader with Wisdom as presented in the book of Proverbs. We will explore Wisdom's story (Chapter One), personality and purpose (Chapter Two) so that we can know Wisdom and begin to mimic Wisdom's ways. Wisdom is communicated through *proverbs,* so we will learn what a proverb is (Chapter Three).

The beginning of the way of Wisdom is the fear of the Lord (Chapter Four). Wisdom comes from outside of us; it is revealed. God's revelation is fundamental to our knowledge of wisdom (Chapter Five), but we must cultivate a heart to receive it (Chapter Six) as we hear it from parents (Chapter Seven) and friends (Chapter Eight). Wisdom is developed through watching and learning (Chapter Nine) from the point at which you first encounter Wisdom (Chapter Ten).

More work remains to be done exploring the benefits of wisdom, the character of wisdom, and how we express wisdom in our attitudes and actions, but, in the spirit of Proverbs, we must be patient, taking time to build a relationship with Wisdom. In the words of Treebeard in *The Lord of the Rings*, "Don't be hasty." Slow meditation will yield great fruit.

My prayer is that this volume and any future volumes will aid you in cultivating a love for Wisdom so that you can delight in God's will and walk in his ways to the glory of his holy name.

Job 28

"Surely there is a mine for silver,
  and a place for gold that they refine.
Iron is taken out of the earth,
  and copper is smelted from the ore.
Man puts an end to darkness
  and searches out to the farthest limit
  the ore in gloom and deep darkness.
He opens shafts in a valley away from where anyone lives;
  they are forgotten by travelers;
  they hang in the air, far away from mankind; they
  swing to and fro.
As for the earth, out of it comes bread,
  but underneath it is turned up as by fire.
Its stones are the place of sapphires,
  and it has dust of gold.
  "That path no bird of prey knows,
  and the falcon's eye has not seen it.
The proud beasts have not trodden it;
  the lion has not passed over it.
"Man puts his hand to the flinty rock
  and overturns mountains by the roots.
He cuts out channels in the rocks,
  and his eye sees every precious thing.
He dams up the streams so that they do not trickle,
  and the thing that is hidden he brings out to light.

1

"But where shall wisdom be found?
　　And where is the place of understanding?
Man does not know its worth,
　　and it is not found in the land of the living.
The deep says, 'It is not in me,'
　　and the sea says, 'It is not with me.'
It cannot be bought for gold,
　　and silver cannot be weighed as its price.
It cannot be valued in the gold of Ophir,
　　in precious onyx or sapphire.
Gold and glass cannot equal it,
　　nor can it be exchanged for jewels of fine gold.
No mention shall be made of coral or of crystal;
　　the price of wisdom is above pearls.
The topaz of Ethiopia cannot equal it,
　　nor can it be valued in pure gold.
"From where, then, does wisdom come?
　　And where is the place of understanding?
It is hidden from the eyes of all living
　　and concealed from the birds of the air.
Abaddon and Death say,
　　'We have heard a rumor of it with our ears.'
"God understands the way to it,
　　and he knows its place.
For he looks to the ends of the earth
　　and sees everything under the heavens.
When he gave to the wind its weight
　　and apportioned the waters by measure,
when he made a decree for the rain
　　and a way for the lightning of the thunder,
then he saw it and declared it;

he established it, and searched it out.
And he said to man,
'Behold, the fear of the Lord, that is wisdom,
 and to turn away from evil is understanding.'"

CHAPTER 1

Searching For Wisdom

Life is pretty simple when you are young. Everything is laid out for you. There are clear rules to follow and very little responsibility. Of course, in your younger years, you think you have the weight of the world on your shoulders. However, you do not think much about your purpose in life or how things are supposed to work. Your mind is on your next meal, game, or homework assignment. The extent of thinking about purpose might be, "Why do I have to take algebra? How is that going to be useful?" but beyond that, you are not thinking much about "the meaning of it all."

The older you grow, however, the more you have to think about how life is supposed to work and its meaning. You begin asking questions, searching. What are you looking for? Wisdom. You are looking for wisdom. Where do you find it? That is Job's question in Job 28.

Job is writing in a context of suffering. He is trying to make sense of it all in the face of his accusers. Job 28 expresses what Job is looking for and his musings on how to find it. Does man find wisdom like he discovers other things in creation? Job speaks of how man has manipulated and discovered many things in the creation: mining the earth for metals and precious metals, demolishing mountains to discover precious things, damming rivers to discover the hidden things in the riverbeds. Where do you go for wisdom? Can you discover it like these other things? Can the world be manipulated so you can dig up this thing or overturn that thing and find wisdom? Can wisdom be bought with gold or silver? No, wisdom is beyond the reach of money. It is far more precious. It is priceless. Job comes to the conclusion that wisdom cannot be found in creation alone. The birds cannot find it in the heavens and death cannot find it in the depths of the earth (Job 28:20-22).

There is a way to find wisdom, but you must have on the proper spectacles: the fear of Yahweh. The world apart from the fear of Yahweh appears random and chaotic; there is no meaning and purpose, no order or unity. Wisdom is the fear of Yahweh, and to turn away from evil is understanding (Job 28:28).

The search for wisdom is a major theme that has led many to associate the book of Job with Proverbs, Ecclesiastes, Song of Songs, and Psalms as wisdom literature. As the label suggests, these books concern wisdom and reveal it: what it is, how it is to be found, and how it is expressed.

Wisdom is about the meaning of life. How does everything work and fit together so as to make sense of the world? Wisdom is about relationships. How does a particular action relate to a particular consequence? How does one event relate to another?

Before digging into the book of Proverbs, we must grasp its context within the biblical genre of wisdom literature and clearly define "wisdom."

First, we must distinguish between God's wisdom and our wisdom. These two are obviously related since all our wisdom is derived from our all-wise God. But our wisdom is not God's wisdom. As I mentioned, wisdom is about relationships. God's wisdom is the knowledge by which he builds and maintains his relationship within himself and with his creation.

God understands how all relationships work. He understands their meaning and purpose. God understands how everything fits together and makes sense. God knows, for example, how evil fits within his good order. He understands how what we perceive as simply chaos is actually part of his good order, for the benefit of his people and creation.

The knowledge of how everything works begins with God's knowledge of himself. We will visit this more in a moment, but God eternally exists in relationship as Father, Son, and Holy Spirit. Each person of the Trinity understands the other in infinite depth. Each member understands the meaning, purpose, and unity of the relationship. Each member knows what it takes to make these relationships work as they ought, and they engage one another in these ways in order to maintain these relationships. Everything in God's relationship as Trinity makes complete sense to him. God has a comprehensive grasp on everything about himself and his relationships.

This is different from our wisdom. Our wisdom is faith that seeks knowledge and conformity to the way God constructs and maintains relationships within himself and with his creation, recognizes the limitations of human knowledge, and submits to divine mystery. We do not have a comprehensive grasp on anything. Our wisdom is that which is derived from God. The only way we understand anything about the meaning of life and how things work in the world is through what God has revealed to us. Even though we have this understanding, we will never be able to comprehend everything.

This characterization of wisdom may be different from your understanding of wisdom. Generally, we think of wisdom as having answers and being able to fix things: Wisdom is "applied knowledge," which many take to mean, "If you have true wisdom, you can figure anything out." We go to a man whom we perceive to be wise because we want him to give us the answers about what financial decision to make, what person to choose as our spouse, what school to attend, why we lost a loved one, or why life has generally fallen to pieces. A wise man, we think, will not only understand these things, but he will somehow fix them.

Wisdom, for many of us, is the ability to control our lives and circumstances. Wisdom becomes a means to human sovereignty. Wisdom is power to control my life. There are elements of truth in this. God certainly wants us to figure out many things about our lives, having a grasp on some things so that we can live certain ways and experience good things, but we will never be all-wise, able to understand and control everything.

"But," some may ask, "if we can't be all-wise, why do we need wisdom at all? Why not live in a perpetual state of simplicity and immaturity? Ignorance is bliss, right?" The answer is that we need wisdom to fulfill our callings as images of God and take dominion over the earth. God does not make it easy for us to figure out everything we may face. The hard labor of discovering what he has concealed is part of the journey to wisdom. We read in Proverbs 25:2, "It is the glory of God to conceal a matter; it is the glory of kings to search a matter out." We are called to make sense of the world, to understand how things fit together as they should, and how people must relate to one another as they should. We need to make sense of the world as much as possible so we can order it properly.

The dominion project is God's great riddle, his dark saying, which he expects us to work at. Solomon wants his son to "understand ... the words of the wise and their riddles" (Prov 1:6). Creation, made and sustained by the word of Wisdom's power (Prov 8; Heb 1:3), is a riddle, a dark saying in which God hides riches that must be searched out (Prov 25:2). We do not live in a simple world ordered only by cause and effect. We live in an enigmatic world. To complete our mission of dominion, we must grow out of our immature simplicity and into wisdom. We must work to build and maintain these proper relationships in the world in ways that are pleasing to God.

We lose true, creaturely wisdom by thinking we can understand everything, and, consequently, thinking that we can control everything. True wisdom involves realizing the limitations of our wisdom.

Wisdom is, above all, the fear of Yahweh. Though this means many things, the fear of Yahweh first acknowledges that I am not the sovereign one, and I do not have–and cannot have–all the answers. While I search, struggle, and wrestle with God for answers, at the end of the day true wisdom might have to say, "I don't have an answer. This makes no sense to me at all. But I trust you, Lord. I know that it all makes sense to you." True wisdom submits to divine mystery, affirming and resting in what God has revealed and leaving to him alone what he has not revealed. A truly wise person can rest in this mystery because they understand God's relationship to creation.

But if God is all-wise, knowing how everything fits together for a good purpose, then each one of his commands has a purpose that fits with his wisdom. It is wise to trust the one who is all-wise even when we do not have a full understanding of the matters at hand. We must trust in Yahweh with all our hearts and lean not on our own understanding; in all our ways we must acknowledge him, and he will direct our paths (Prov 3:5-6).

In Scripture, the fool is just the opposite of the wise man. He is the one who says, "No," to God (Psa 14:1). He refuses to operate in God's world in the way that he designed it. He kicks against God at every turn even though he enjoys the benefits of God's wisdom. The fool may have much in the way of intellectual capacity and book learning, but because he does not submit to God, he cannot see things the way they really are. God has called us away from our foolishness, which is nothing more than rebellion.

Our loving heavenly Father has set us on the quest for wisdom. He wants us to search out matters. Solomon leads his son in his initial quest to answer Job's question, "But where shall wisdom be found?" Wisdom has a story. When we comprehend that story, we can safely set out on the treacherous journey to discover Wisdom.

Wisdom's Beginnings and Progress In Eternity

Wisdom's story does not begin with humanity. Wisdom is not fundamentally humanity's attempt to understand God and the world around him. Wisdom is intrinsic to God himself. It is who he is.

Proverbs 8 tells the story of creation from Wisdom's perspective. Wisdom was there before the creation. Yahweh possessed Wisdom in the beginning, before the worlds were made, and Wisdom was "daily his delight" (Prov 8:30). Wisdom was the joy of God before there was a world. Wisdom is a person.

It is true that Solomon is using a literary technique that we would call personification. But wisdom is not an abstraction. Wisdom is not a bodiless thought that floats around and comes to rest in people here and there. Wisdom is not something that can be separated from people and their relationships, or quantified scientifically, as though by an impersonal computer. Wisdom is personal. Wisdom is the relationships between persons, not some disembodied philosophy or theory.

So, while we may say that Solomon is personifying wisdom, we must not think of his characterization as merely literary. Wisdom is personal and is, indeed, a person. When Yahweh delights in Wisdom before the beginning,

11

he is delighting in a person. The reason he can do this is because he exists eternally as Father, Son, and Spirit.

God is eternally in relationship. God exists in three persons. He is not a monad. This relationship between the persons of the Trinity is Wisdom. There could be no Wisdom if there were not a Trinity. Wisdom is a matter of understanding how this over here relates to that over there, and how they all work together for meaning and purpose. Wisdom shows how many things relate to one another in unity. The basis for Wisdom is the eternal relationship between the Father, Son, and Spirit who is both many and one, relating perfectly with one another.

These relationships exist eternally. The Father eternally delights in the Son, the Son in the Father, the Father in the Spirit, the Spirit in the Father, the Son in the Spirit, and the Spirit in the Father. The Father understands the Son infinitely, comprehensively. He knows what is best for the Son and how to achieve that. He delights to relate to him in these ways. This makes their relationship "work" and fulfills the meaning and purpose of their existence. Reciprocally, the Son understands what is best in his relationship with the Father, and relates to the Father in those ways. So it goes in the eternal, divine dance of Wisdom.

That knowledge of one another, that understanding of how these relationships work, is the infinite wisdom of God. God's Wisdom within himself is his infinite understanding of how his own relationships work, what makes sense, and what their meaning is.

In Creation

Enter the creation. God establishes a new relationship. When he created the world, God did so by wisdom and in wisdom. Proverbs 3:19 says, "Yahweh by wisdom founded the earth; by understanding he established the heavens" (see also Jer 10:12; 51:15; Psa 104:24). Proverbs 8 speaks in detail about how it was by Wisdom that God created the world. Solomon presents Wisdom as the Architect of creation. Wisdom was the "master craftsman" (Prov 8:30). Wisdom designed the world. In doing so, Wisdom put its indelible impression on the entire world.

Wisdom was not only the Architect but also, in some way, the blueprint for the world. The world was designed according to Wisdom's design, and Wisdom's design was found in Wisdom himself. We might say it this way: the world was made in the image of Wisdom. Everything in the world has the impression of God's Wisdom on it.

As one author says, "According to Proverbs it was by wisdom that Yahweh founded the earth (Prov 3:19). The result is that his wisdom is woven into the warp and woof of the very fabric of creation."[1] The world, in all its relationships and parts, bears the image of God's Wisdom. The world's template for relationships is in God himself. Our relationships are to be like God's relationships. That is how we make sense of the world.

---

1. Craig G. Bartholomew, Ryan P. O'Dowd, *Old Testament Wisdom Literature: A Theological Introduction* (Westmont, Illinois: IVP Academic, 2011), 16.

The creation cannot be understood apart from God's Wisdom. This is why the fear of Yahweh is the beginning of knowledge and wisdom (Prov 1:7; 9:10). If you want to understand the world properly, the first thing you must do is submit yourself—your intellect and everything else that you are—to the Creator. What we learn when we look at our Triune Creator is that the world is supposed to operate in a way where there is love, unity, purpose, and mutual self-giving. This is what we call reality. This is the way the world operates, the way God created and sustains the world. To oppose God's wisdom is to defy reality, like calling boys "girls" and girls "boys," thinking you can live in sin with impunity, thinking a society can live or thrive in defiance to God's laws.

In the Garden

Wisdom's operations in the world took a horrible turn in the beginning of the creation. The apex of Wisdom's creation was in man himself—God's image. Man was created to relate to God according to Wisdom. However, while God created man in Wisdom, man himself was created immature and would have to grow up into this wisdom.

It was as though God had a crown and some clothes for man to wear that were too large for him when he was created. He would have to grow up to fit the clothes. We know this from Scripture. Man's movement is to be from one stage of glory to another, from immaturity to maturity.

When we read the Garden story through the lens of what comes later in Scripture, we can see how this was God's determination from the beginning, even before the fall. God created the Garden and placed man in it. Every tree of the Garden was to be food for man, at least eventually (Gen 1:29). God specified two trees in the Garden in his instructions to man: the Tree of Life and the Tree of the Knowledge of Good and Evil.

From the Tree of Life, man was initially free to eat. There was never a prohibition against eating from the Tree of Life before the fall. It is at least implied by the name God gave the Tree that this was precisely where Adam was to go and eat. He was to realize that his life came from God, and he was to seek that life at the place God appointed: in the midst of the Garden at the Tree of Life.

The other Tree was forbidden, for the time being. God said in Genesis 1:29 that every tree would be food for them. The prohibition against eating from the Tree of Knowledge of Good and Evil was a temporary prohibition. When we look through the Scripture, we find that the phrase "the knowledge of good and evil" (and similar phrases) has a specific reference to people who have the ability to make mature judgments. These are the people who have grown up, beyond the simple rules of black-and-white do's and don'ts, have the ability to discern matters that are not so clear. Such people make judgments that incur consequences of life and death.

When you are a small child, your parents will tell you, "Don't go out in the street." That is a clear rule you must not violate. Everything for the small child is nice, neat, and tidy. Clear lines. But when you grow older, you know that this rule does not apply in the same way. The heart of the rule that seeks to keep you from danger is still in place. You should not be foolhardy, playing fast and loose with your life in the street. But as a grown up, you have to go out into the street. You also must exercise discernment about what kind of activity to engage in while in the street, whether good or not good. The choice is not as clear-cut as when you were a child. You must have mature discernment, knowing that your decisions have life-and-death consequences.

Mature discernment is at the heart of the phrase "knowledge of good and evil." The man and the woman had a basic understanding of right and wrong. They knew they should not eat from the Tree. That was a clear rule. But they did not have the "knowledge of good and evil." That only comes with maturity. That is wisdom.

Moses describes the generation of Israel that went through the wilderness and was able to enter the Promised Land as those who, when this journey started, were unable to discern good and evil (Deut 1:39). That particular generation included all those people under twenty years of age (Num 14:29). They knew the difference between right and wrong, but they were not mature. When David was asked by a woman to rule in her case, he was praised as an angel of God who was able to discern between good and evil (2 Sam 14:17). When Solomon prayed that famous prayer asking for wisdom, he realized he was young and did not have the ability to judge between good and evil (1 Kings 3:7-9). As king, he needed the knowledge of good and evil to bring justice to people. The author of Hebrews refers to this relationship between maturity and the knowledge of good and evil in terms of food: "But solid food is for the mature, for those who have their powers of discernment trained by constant practice to distinguish good from evil" (Heb 5:14). The mature are able to eat the food of the knowledge of good and evil. Circumstances would have been the same for Adam and Eve, eventually. When they grew up and had their "powers of discernment trained by constant practice," they could have eaten the "solid food" of the Tree of Knowledge of Good and Evil. Then they would have been able to assume greater responsibility, the responsibility to rule as king and queen.

But they were impatient. Man's sin was grasping for this position before the time (something that is characteristic of most, if not all, sin). We are constantly reaching for things that God has put beyond our grasp for the present. If we will just be patient, God will give us these things at the appropriate time—the time when he deems that we are ready for them.

After they ate the fruit, God declares that the man "has become like one of us in knowing good and evil." Man assumes this position of rule, and this development is not a good thing at that particular time. It is sinful and corrupts man completely. Consequently, God exiles him from the Garden, keeping him away from the Tree of Life, lest he eat and live forever.

Man's purpose, however, did not change. He continues to be called to mature and gain wisdom so he may rule with wisdom as king over God's creation—a reality ultimately seen in Jesus Christ.

In Israel

God's plans and purposes did not end with the fall of man. Man would grow up in Wisdom. The life of the people of God reflects this progress of wisdom.

Man begins immature with a clear set of rules. This is just how our lives begin. There is not much room for discernment. Here is the rule for this and this and this. The world is a world of clear cause-and-effect. Do this, and you will be praised. Do this, and you will be punished. Everything is clear. This is what childhood is.

God's people Israel began as children. They were the new Adam, freshly created, as it were, and immature. Through Moses, God gave them many, many rules. They had all sorts of rules concerning worship, uncleanness, how to be cleansed, what to do with pots when lizards fell into them, and more.

Rules for everything. Life was simple in many ways. But they had to grow up. And they did. This new wine of maturity was bursting the old wineskin of childhood. A world of simple cause-and-effect or black-and-white rules was no longer sufficient.

Sure, there were still things that were clearly sin. There were clear lines of obedience and disobedience. But not everything worked like it did when they were younger. They would have to apply those rules in different ways just like you do now when you go to the street.

To put it in more biblical categories, life begins as a priest. Basic responsibilities are, fear God and do this. You are a worshiper fundamentally. You are not created *homo sapien* (wise man). You are created *homo adorans* (worshiping man). You are to be content with that priestly stage of life while you are in it, but you are to press on to maturity. That next stage of maturity is to be a king.

As a king you are called to make grown-up judgments about life and death. You are to discern how the rules you learned in childhood apply or do not apply, depending on various situations. You do not have a rule for everything. You have to figure out some things based on the fundamentals you learned in childhood.

This is where the wisdom books fall in Israel's history. They were written by kings, about kings and how they are to rule. Israel has grown up into a kingdom with a king who relates to the nations differently than before. What Israel's king discovers is that life is not so easy anymore. You might hear people say, or have yourself said, "Life was so much simpler when we were children." Yes, it was. But to try to return to that period instead of growing up as God has called is sinful.

Israel and her king were to wrestle with the world and discover what God had hidden. They were to figure out, as much as possible, how everything was to relate properly and what God was teaching them from the creation about his wisdom. Since we know that God created the world and sustains it in Wisdom, and since we fear Yahweh, we can look through those lenses and see the impress of wisdom on the ant and the locust and learn from them about self-disciplined determination and order, just as Solomon teaches us in Proverbs. We are learning how the world works, and through this we accomplish our mission to subdue the world for God's glory.

One of the painful and often frustrating realities of the kingly stage is that our wisdom falls short. We cannot comprehend everything. But that too, as we learn from Ecclesiastes, is actually a blessing. We can rest in the One who has control over everything. Job, Psalms, Proverbs, Ecclesiastes, and Song of Songs each represent a part of this stage in Israel's history. This is the time of kings, so it is the time for wisdom.

In us

Wisdom's story does not stop there. It progresses and is fulfilled in Christ to whom all judgment has been given by the Father. He patiently endured and was crowned king. Now, we in Christ are a "grown up" church that is still looking, as Paul says, to grow up into a mature man (Eph 4:12, 15). We are to grow up in Wisdom.

In your creation as a human, you are designed by the Wisdom of God and in it. God's Wisdom is part of who you are as his created image. Now re-created in Christ Jesus, that image is renewed in you. Being re-created in Christ means that we are set on a journey toward greater wisdom.

The first stage of discovering wisdom in our lives is plainly taught to us by Job and echoed by Solomon: Wisdom is the fear of Yahweh, the fear of the Lord Jesus (Job 28:28; Prov 9:10). You begin accepting how God has defined you, what he declares you to be and what he requires of you. You submit to his Word, his Wisdom. This is nothing more than faith. You accept what God says as true and you conform your life to it.

Your life as a king never leaves the priestly stage in one sense: you remain a worshiper. Worship with the people of God around Word and Sacrament is headquarters in the quest for wisdom. Without corporate worship as the heart of your life, you will never get wisdom. You will never really comprehend how the world works properly. You will submit to the enemy's lies. Your priestly life of worship is absolutely necessary in your search for wisdom.

While we never leave the fear of Yahweh, we do grow up in it. Growing in wisdom is our aim in meditating on and learning the book of Proverbs.

God has called us to this search for wisdom. He has called us to mature. We begin by our basic confession that we fear Yahweh and keep his commandments (Eccl 12:13). That will be our wisdom as we make new discoveries as well as when we cannot figure out everything and must submit to divine mystery.

Proverbs 8

Does not wisdom call?
  Does not understanding raise her voice?
On the heights beside the way,
  at the crossroads she takes her stand;
beside the gates in front of the town,
  at the entrance of the portals she cries aloud:
"To you, O men, I call,
  and my cry is to the children of man.
O simple ones, learn prudence;
  O fools, learn sense.
Hear, for I will speak noble things,
  and from my lips will come what is right,
for my mouth will utter truth;
  wickedness is an abomination to my lips.
All the words of my mouth are righteous;
  there is nothing twisted or crooked in them.
They are all straight to him who understands,
  and right to those who find knowledge.
Take my instruction instead of silver,
  and knowledge rather than choice gold,
for wisdom is better than jewels,
  and all that you may desire cannot compare with her.
"I, wisdom, dwell with prudence,
  and I find knowledge and discretion.
The fear of Yahweh is hatred of evil.

Pride and arrogance and the way of evil
  and perverted speech I hate.
I have counsel and sound wisdom;
  I have insight; I have strength.
By me kings reign,
  and rulers decree what is just;
by me princes rule,
  and nobles, all who govern justly.
I love those who love me,
  and those who seek me diligently find me.
Riches and honor are with me,
  enduring wealth and righteousness.
My fruit is better than gold, even fine gold,
  and my yield than choice silver.
I walk in the way of righteousness,
  in the paths of justice,
granting an inheritance to those who love me,
  and filling their treasuries.
Yahweh possessed me at the beginning of his work,
  the first of his acts of old.
Ages ago I was set up,
  at the first, before the beginning of the earth.
When there were no depths I was brought forth,
  when there were no springs abounding with water.
Before the mountains had been shaped,
  before the hills, I was brought forth,
before he had made the earth with its fields,
  or the first of the dust of the world.
When he established the heavens, I was there;
  when he drew a circle on the face of the deep,
when he made firm the skies above,

when he established the fountains of the deep,
when he assigned to the sea its limit,
* so that the waters might not transgress his command,*
when he marked out the foundations of the earth,
then I was beside him, like a master workman,
and I was daily his delight,
* rejoicing before him always,*
rejoicing in his inhabited world
* and delighting in the children of man.*
And now, O sons, listen to me:
* blessed are those who keep my ways.*
* Hear instruction and be wise,*
* and do not neglect it.*
Blessed is the one who listens to me,
* watching daily at my gates,*
* waiting beside my doors.*
For whoever finds me finds life
* and obtains favor from Yaweh,*
but he who fails to find me injures himself;
* all who hate me love death."*

CHAPTER 2

Living Wisdom

We live in a messy world. Some of the mess is built into creation, like the original chaotic, unformed, and unfilled creation in Genesis 1:1-2. Creation, even before the Fall, needed to be sorted out and put in order. Sin intensifies the mess and confuses our calling to order the creation. The task that God has given to the children of man is difficult, as Solomon says in Ecclesiastes 1:13. The world does not operate in a simple cause-and-effect relationship all of the time. The world is much more complicated than that. God has called us to grow up in wisdom so that we can handle these more complicated issues and do the work he has created and called us to do.

Wisdom understands relationships: how this thing over here fits with that thing over there to create something that is true, beautiful, good, harmonious, and peaceful. Wisdom touches everything from art to interpersonal human relationships, from the construction of buildings to building societies. God has called us to grow in wisdom so we can fulfill our purpose as man.

The fundamental of all wisdom is the fear of the Lord. We are not God and will never have all wisdom. True wisdom begins by submitting to the wisdom of God who understands all relationships comprehensively from the beginning to the end and everything in between. He knows how everything works together for one good purpose.

Wisdom is personal

As seen in Proverbs 8, Wisdom is portrayed as a person. Like any person there are certain personality characteristics. The first and most obvious characteristic is that *Wisdom is personal.*

As mentioned in Chapter One, wisdom has to do with knowledge of relationships of all kinds but especially human relationships. The funny thing about human relationships is that they are, in many ways, unpredictable. People change. Situations for people change, requiring responses you may not have anticipated. People are not machines into which we can simply plug a formulaic answer and make everything start functioning as designed.

Wisdom itself reveals to us its personal nature. It is not mechanical. Wisdom considers context and does not simply give pat answers to every situation that looks remotely similar. One of the obvious passages in Proverbs that reflects this truth is in 26:4, 5: "Answer not a fool according to his folly, lest you be like him yourself. Answer a fool according to his folly, lest he be wise in his own eyes." The simple man hears this proverb and says, "Well, which is it, Solomon? Should I answer the fool according to his folly or not?"

Wisdom considers the situation. Wisdom takes into account your relationship with the other person, how much time you have invested in the relationship, whether the person is belligerent or teachable, and many other factors.

Proverbs can easily be misused (just as the rest of Scripture). The Proverbs are terse, salty, generally unqualified statements that seem (at least on the surface) to have a simple cause-and-effect relationship. For example, Proverbs 10:30 reads, "The righteous will never be removed, but the wicked will not dwell in the land." Taken without qualification, the proverb could be interpreted, "If you are removed from the land, then that must mean you are wicked. The wicked never retain the land."

We know this interpretation is not true in every situation in life. Ultimately, the proverb is true, but there are times in history where just the opposite happens. Jesus is crucified outside the city gates and the wicked continue to dwell in the land. We know their fortunes were eventually reversed, but how would you apply the proverb to Jesus' situation in AD 30? That is, how would you apply it when you are going through the situation, when you do not have the leisure of a bigger historical picture? The simple may repeat these proverbs and apply them incorrectly, such as saying something which is right but at the wrong time. Bumper sticker theology will not carry one through life. Context matters.

We are not machines. Spouting a verse as though it fits each and every situation requires little to no effort. You do not really have to consider the person and their story. But Wisdom requires that we consider the person and his situation and apply Scripture correctly. Proverbs speaks to this when it says, "To make an apt answer is a joy to a man, and a word in season, how good it is!" (15:23). It is beautiful when a person says the right thing at the right time: "A word fitly spoken is like apples of gold in a setting of silver." (25:11)

Consider this: the Scriptures are a source of great comfort for us in times of despair and tragedy, but misused in a simplistic, superficial fashion they can become destructive. Wisdom is familiar with the Scriptures and knows how to use them at the appropriate times in the appropriate ways. Yes, there are some basic principles that apply to situations across the board. But simply quoting a verse without considering the person and their situation could be cruel. If you walk into a funeral parlor where people are mourning the loss of a loved one, you don't enter and proclaim, "Well, you know, Philippians 4:4 says, 'Rejoice in the Lord always, again I will say, Rejoice!'" Does the Scripture command us to rejoice? Yes. Is it correct? Yes. Is it appropriate for that time? No. The Scripture also has quite a bit to say about mourning. Jesus himself mourned at the grave of Lazarus (John 11:35).

Wisdom is personal, taking into account the whole life situation. It does not simply give pat answers to difficult questions.

Wisdom is productive

Another trait of Wisdom is its *productivity*. Interestingly, the first mention of the word "wisdom" in Scripture is in the context of God giving men the skills they need to build the Tabernacle. God appoints Moses to speak to all the skillful men whom he has given the Spirit of wisdom so they might make Aaron's garments for the priesthood (Exod 28:3). Bezalel and Oholiab are two artisans who have oversight of the construction of the Tabernacle, and they have wisdom (Exod 31:2-11; 35:30-35). They obtain wisdom to make things, to be productive. Wisdom involves skills. Wisdom itself is, Proverbs 8:30 says, a "master craftsman." Wisdom can see how things ought to fit together in a way that creates good order and beauty.

The specific focus of wisdom and its productivity is clear: it is given in order to build the house of God. This is the place where God will dwell and meet with his people. We know the entire creation project is a project whose focus is to build the house of God. The creation is to be patterned after heaven, the house of God, just like the Tabernacle. God gave this task to man when he created him. Man was to be fruitful, multiply, fill the earth, and subdue it. For man to fulfill this task, he would need the Spirit of Wisdom who created everything to begin with. The Spirit grants wisdom to God's people in all of their culture-building activities.

The skills you learn and apply in your vocation on a day-by-day basis are God's gifts of wisdom to you. You have skills to put together information and use that information for the purposes of productivity. This is a part of that house-building project to which God has called his people.

While wisdom involves working with non-human objects, we also know that God's house-building project involves humans as well. The Tabernacle and the Temple that followed it were both symbols of the living reality of God's people. Wisdom involves building up one another.

Paul uses this imagery in 1 Corinthians 3, where he incorporates language that echoes Proverbs 8 and images of Bezalel and Oholiab. Paul is a "wise master builder" who lays the foundation and builds upon it the Temple of God, the church. This church is made up of living stones, as Peter says. It is a house built by the Spirit and for the Spirit (i.e., "a spiritual house," 1 Pet 2:5). The mission of the people of God is to build a house, using people as its materials. Jesus speaks about the project as "discipling the nations."

When Jesus poured out his Spirit on the church on the Day of Pentecost, he was commissioning and enabling us to be master craftsmen to complete this Temple-building project. We are, each one of us, Bezalel and Oholiab in some way. The problem with living stones is that they do not always cooperate. They are fidgety. Their shape seems to be constantly changing so that they do not stay in place. It takes wisdom—people filled by the Spirit—to build God's house. This does not only concern what we call the vocational Christian ministry (pastors, teachers, missionaries). Each one of us has a great responsibility in this task, and we must be examples of Spirit-filled wisdom to everyone else, but wisdom is also about how you shape your job situations to make them and the rest of the world look a little more like heaven.

How is what you are doing—whether in the medical field, at the factory, construction, information technology, or whatever you do—reflecting the order and beauty of God? When you serve others with your product or service, is it making their lives more productive, bringing them rest, bringing them enjoyment and satisfaction? How are you working with other people, in your vocation, to minister to them? How are you building your relationships with them? Are you seeking to make these relationships what they ought to be, even if the other person does not reciprocate? All these considerations are involved in wisdom's productivity. Wisdom goes about trying to build and maintain God's desired order in the world.

Wisdom is puzzling

A third trait of wisdom is that it is *puzzling*. Challenges arise when we seek to employ wisdom. As I said, people do not always stay in place like bricks and wood. People are puzzling, so wisdom is sometimes puzzling as well. Wisdom invites you into mysteries in order to unravel them and put them back together in the proper way.

In Solomon's opening words to his son in Proverbs 1, he speaks of life's situations as riddles or enigmas: "Let the wise hear and increase in learning, and the one who understands obtain guidance, to understand a proverb and a saying, the words of the wise and their riddles" (1:5-6). Proverbs and the words of the wise are riddles, mysteries. This is not the simple world of cliché answers and easy decisions between what is clearly sin and what is clearly not. We should already be making the right decisions in those areas. These riddles go beyond that. These are the paradoxes of life: those things that are apparent contradictions but they are not contradictions.

Paradoxes throw the purely logical mind into confusion. Everything is supposed to work in simple syllogisms, unalterably. Anyone who has lived long enough knows this logical formula does not match the vicissitudes of life.

This tension was illustrated quite well in the movie *I, Robot* (2004). In this story, scientists create artificial intelligence that works strictly by laws of logic: "the Three Laws." The main computer that controls all the individual robots, V.I.K.I, created to serve humans, decides it is logical to imprison humans in their homes to protect them from one another. V.I.K.I.'s logic, it says, is undeniable. At one level this is true. Humans are destroying themselves. But the situation is much more complicated than what the most complex computer may determine by using formulas.

In the early 2020s, we faced the challenges sparked by the COVID-19 virus, and the resulting dilemmas for church and society tested even the wisest of minds, especially in the beginning. We were forced to ask questions like, "How much risk is wise to take in the face of a novel virus?" There were complex situations, but for many people, the whole of life was survival, and survival at all costs. To survive, we must isolate, shut down businesses, etc. But after months of this behavior, people began wondering whether "survival" alone was satisfactory. Trying to survive the virus through lockdowns had economic and mental health consequences that created more devastation than the virus itself.

To make decisions like those made during the COVID-19 pandemic—even in imperfect situations—you need leaders who have wisdom, people who understand proper trade-offs between risk and reward, who take into account more than one aspect of a situation, and who are willing to live with the negative consequences that will inevitably occur.

The wisest of decisions do not give you complete leverage of the situation so that everything turns out the way everyone desires, at least in the short-run. The world operates with paradoxes that frustrate simple logic. We know things to be "bittersweet." Logically speaking, A cannot be A and non-A at the same time and in the same relationship. But life is sometimes bittersweet. We know how things can be both bitter and sweet at the same time. We know how what is bad in one sense can also be good at the same time in another sense. The death of a loved one who has suffered agony for a long time is bittersweet. Leaving friends, family, or a loved geographical region for new opportunities is bittersweet. The cross of Christ is bittersweet in this way. It is the great paradox and the wisdom of God. This one situation reflects the appalling consequences of sin and the great mercy of God. This is the material with which wisdom works and the world in which it lives.

However, these riddles are not all incomprehensible. Solomon is writing the book to his son so that his son may understand a proverb and enigmas or riddles. Solomon wants his son to "increase in learning," "obtain guidance," and "to understand" proverbs and riddles. We know from Job and Ecclesiastes there are limits on our human wisdom. There are some riddles we will never solve. We cannot, as

Ecclesiastes says, "shepherd the wind" and shape the mist, or vapor. Ultimately, we do not have control over anything because we are not all-wise. But God has given us some wisdom. What ability we have to shape the mist is the gracious gift of God.

You will not go to Wisdom Literature and obtain a precise instruction manual about how to deal with every situation. Wisdom will be a struggle with all situations in life, especially those in which there are no clear answers. Sometimes we must muddle our way through it.

Wisdom is poetic

Wisdom is not only puzzling but *poetic*. The form Wisdom takes in these books is poetry, not prose. Poetry uses images that are multifaceted. Poetry is, what we might call, "concentrated language." It is pregnant brevity. It bursts at the seams with meaning, implications, and applications.

The fullness of this poetic style is revealed through literary devices like parallelisms. Biblical poets will write things once and either repeat the same thing with different words or contrast it with an opposite idea. For the precisionist, poetry is too messy because it is too open-ended and embellished. It leaves too many loose ends and is a waste of words. "Just say it clearly in black-and-white and move on," the precise person says. Wisdom's poetry makes sure you hear the complexity of the situation. It is not adequate to say something only once. It must be said, and it must be said again, embellished in some way.

We hear it in Proverbs 8 in the opening words: "Does not wisdom call? / Does not understanding raise her voice? (8:1).

Then again in Proverbs 8:5, "O simple ones, learn prudence; / O fools, learn sense."

In each of these instances what is said in the first line is repeated in the second line but by using different words.

Sometimes one thing is said and its opposite is emphasized in a parallel fashion, just to make sure you do not miss the point. For instance, returning to Proverbs 8, we read, "For whoever finds me finds life and obtains favor from Yahweh, but he who fails to find me injures himself; all who hate me love death." (Prov 8:35-36). The language, like Wisdom itself, is beautiful and mysterious. The proverb reflects the rhythms of life and expresses the author's wonder, especially in a world where logic and precision are sometimes not only not needed but inadequate.

Life is not written in strict, precise prose with everything in neat and tidy categories. There is surprise and mystery. There is pain too deep for words and joy that cannot be contained by words. Sometimes only weeping and laughter can express these realities. Words fail. Rigid and analytical language cannot capture all aspects of human experience.

There is wisdom in poetry, though. Poetry can disclose wisdom because poetry works within restraints and yet poetry resists exhaustive description. Many times, we want to tame the language by making it more precise. There is nothing necessarily wrong with precision in language. Sometimes precision is needed and called for. But we must be careful. We must know that wisdom cannot be controlled like that.

Craig Bartholomew and Ryan O'Dowd say it this way:

> Today poetry is, very often, our truest link with reality. Our modern age has tended to prefer facts and reason to imagination. Such an emphasis can misrepresent, underestimate, flatten and distort reality. To say that God is "transcendent" or "omniscient," while it has noble aims, is qualitatively different than declaring that God rules "the raging sea" (Psa 89:9) or asking, "Can you draw in Leviathan with a hook?" (Job 41:1). Both are appropriate for different contexts, but one is not more "true." In this way, biblical poetry alerts us to the limitations of abstract language. Poetry, in fact, is at its best an ethical way of preserving the mystery, ambiguity, power, tragedy, and sublimity of our world.[1]

The form and words of wisdom in Scripture reflect its nature. Just when you think you have a handle on the energetic beast, you find the leash ripped from your hands and the bars of your precision ripped open. This is, it seems to me, the reason why God's wisdom is expressed in poetic form. Wisdom is complex, beautiful, multi-dimensional, uncontainable, and mysterious. Yet God in his grace gives us some handles on it so that we can operate his world.

---

1. Bartholomew, Craig G. & Ryan O'Dowd, *Old Testament Wisdom Literature: A Theological Introduction* (Downers Grove, IL: IVP Academic, 2011), 69.

Wisdom is a Person

All the traits of Wisdom we have discussed are personality traits: Wisdom is a *Person*.

Proverbs 8 portrays Wisdom as a Person. We know from what the Scriptures say, after the revelation of Christ, that Wisdom is Christ himself. In him, Paul says, are hidden all the treasures of wisdom (Col 2:3). To the Corinthians Paul says Jesus has become for us "the wisdom of God" (1 Cor 1:30). So, unlike Solomon, we now see the fullness of Wisdom. We grasp the way God works in the world better than Solomon did in his time.

If you want to understand the way everything fits together in the world, you must look at Christ. He is the revelation of the Wisdom of God. He *is* the wisdom of God who became *for us* the wisdom of God. In him the world finds its true and intended order. When we look at the life of Christ, we see how God governs his world and how he expects man to govern in his world. Jesus reveals how things were operating all along. He is the secret wisdom that is now revealed in its fullness. In him we see and live the way we ought to live. God's wisdom is a crucified messiah. God's wisdom is living and ruling by giving yourself for others, not insisting on your rights simply because they are your rights, but using your rights to lay down your life for others.

This is God's Wisdom. And that Wisdom is Jesus.

Wisdom's Purpose

Why do I need to pursue wisdom? If it is something that I will never master, why pursue it? There are a number of reasons we ought to pursue wisdom.

First, we are clearly instructed by God to get wisdom. God says through Solomon's instruction to his son, "Get wisdom; get insight; do not forget, and do not turn away from the words of my mouth....The beginning of wisdom is this: Get wisdom, and whatever you get, get insight." (Prov 4:5, 7). Even if we do not understand why, we should trust the all-wise God who knows what is best for us, who never gives us empty pursuits.

Second, pursuing wisdom concerns our ever-deepening relationship with God. Remember that Wisdom, above all things, is a Person, and that Person is Christ Jesus himself. Our God has a personal relationship with us. He relates to us as persons. Relationships between persons are never static. We never master relationships with one another. We come to know one another better, but we never master knowledge of the other person. Pursuing wisdom is about a persevering, growing relationship with God. It is not about achieving a certain degree at which point we can say, "Well, I've obtained that Doctorate of Wisdom, so I can move on with my life to something else." It is about staying in relationship with God and knowing him better. Just because you will never know him comprehensively does not mean you should stop pursuing the relationship. The journey, in some way, is the point of the whole thing. The journey is the gift.

For example, you will never know your spouse comprehensively because we are always growing and changing over time. That does not mean you should stop pursuing a relationship with your spouse. You pursue the relationship and want to maintain it because you love your spouse. The same could be said with parents, children, friends, and other family members. Love pursues wisdom because wisdom is all about knowing the other person.

Third, we need to pursue wisdom because we have a mission *to create*. Wisdom, we learned, is a master craftsman (Prov 8:30). The Spirit of Wisdom hovered over the world in the beginning for this purpose. This same Spirit of Wisdom enabled Bezalel, Oholiab, and Paul to build the house of God. God did not save us just so we could escape hell. Of course, that is a great benefit. But salvation is a call to participate in the life of God himself. We are called to join with him in his mission. We pursue wisdom because we are participating in the life-mission of God. We participate in a creation project that requires the wisdom of God.

Created and re-created as the image of God, work is a part of what it means to be human. If you want to live, if you want to fulfill your purpose as man (and, consequently, to be "fulfilled"), you must work. Work requires wisdom. Your creative, productive work has a purpose, and that purpose is to put things in proper relationship so that there is harmony, joy, beauty, and peace. In order to create these relationships with inanimate objects as well as in interpersonal relationships in your home or on the job, you need wisdom.

Fourth, we pursue wisdom because we are called *to rule*. We are seated with Christ in heavenly places far above all principalities and powers (Eph 1, 2). We are called to rule with Christ in fulfillment of God's original purpose, making decisions that can result in life or death. To rule as we ought, we need wisdom so we may place in order our personal lives, our family, the church, and, if called to it, the larger society around us.

Wisdom is needed by kings. Proverbs 8:15 says, "By me [Wisdom] kings reign." People who rule require more than a simple set of rules to follow. People are messy. We need wisdom to handle the responsibilities God has given to us. We cannot rule well without wisdom, so it must be pursued.

Wisdom is, as mentioned, concerned about relationships with people. We are called to build people. We must pursue wisdom because we love people. We understand that we cannot handle them like computers. Wisdom loves and is, therefore, personal. Since we are called to love people we must pursue wisdom.

Last, we must pursue wisdom because *God has called us to mature*, to grow up to be like him. All of what I have said, in one way or another, is about our maturity. God wants us to grow up and be conformed to the image of Christ who is Wisdom (Rom 8:29). To grow up in Christ is to grow in wisdom. We pursue wisdom because pursuing wisdom is nothing more than speaking about our continuing, growing life as a Christian.

So, in the words of Solomon, "Get wisdom." That is our aim as we study the themes of Proverbs.

Proverbs 1:1-6

The proverbs of Solomon, son of David, king of Israel:

To know wisdom and instruction,
*   to understand words of insight,*
to receive instruction in wise dealing,
*   in righteousness, justice, and equity;*
to give prudence to the simple,
*   knowledge and discretion to the youth—*
Let the wise hear and increase in learning,
*   and the one who understands obtain guidance,*
to understand a proverb and a saying,
*   the words of the wise and their riddles.*

CHAPTER 3

Proverbs: The Catechism of Princes

As man, like Adam, we have a God-given mission in the world. God gave us responsibility to take dominion over the world, creating, ordering, and building a world-house that looks like heaven so that God and man may dwell in it. This is a multi-generational project. So, as we grow older, having done our part and learning a little more of how to fulfill our mission faithfully, we must pass the project to our sons along with the wisdom we have learned.

This is what Solomon is doing in the book of Proverbs. Solomon opens the book by giving it a title: "The proverbs of Solomon." But what is a proverb?

What is a Proverb?

The root of the Hebrew word, "proverb," suggests a comparison. A proverb is what we might call a simile or a metaphor. A proverb is analogy, drawing from one aspect of life and relating it to another aspect of life. A proverb can be a short, pithy statement, or it can be an extended story.

Parables, for example, are proverbs. Jesus, the true Solomon, comes speaking of the kingdom of God in proverbs. The kingdom of God is like leaven, a grain of mustard seed, or a hidden treasure. These analogies assume that all creation is interrelated. How can I learn something from an ant or locusts if their way of living in this world is totally disconnected from mine? The world is all interrelated because it has one purpose created by a single creator. Solomon understands there is a deep structure of relationships in the world that meaningfully inform one another.

In Proverbs 1:6, Solomon compares proverbs with the "sayings of the wise." The wise see these deep, interconnected relationships and bring out principles of wisdom for how we are to live. These relationships show us what to do and what not to do. They instruct us because God has set them up as our teachers. We learn about our relationship to God, one another, and all creation through the way God created and sustains his creation.

These metaphors, analogies, or symbols are woven into the creation from the beginning. Sun, moon, and stars, for instance, are not merely lights in the firmament, though they are that. They are, in biblical symbolism, rulers who determine times and seasons (Gen 1:14). In the Bible, the luminaries correspond to nations and their rulers. This is why Abraham's children will be as the stars in the heavens (Gen 15:5), or why Jacob does not flinch in understanding how the sun, moon, and stars in Joseph's dream refer to Jacob, his wife, and his twelve sons (Gen 37:9-11).

The role of the luminaries as rulers is a revealed metaphor in Scripture. Such metaphors indicate a pattern: there are more relationships in Scripture and in the world, which are intended for our instruction. God has hidden metaphors. We are to search them out. The book of Proverbs does that.

Many people do not think this deeply about the book of Proverbs. In fact, they like Proverbs because it is "practical" and not "theological." Proverbs is not like Leviticus with all the details about the Tabernacle worship system or like Paul's letter to the Romans with all his deep theology. Proverbs deals with everyday life. It is the blue-collar book of the Bible. If we are not careful, however, we may tend to separate all these books according to unbiblical criteria; that is, we may treat the book of Proverbs as though practical matters are more important than spiritual or theological ones.

As we learned earlier, the Spirit of Wisdom created the material world and sustains it. The Spirit of Wisdom also empowers us as co-laborers with God to shape the material aspects of the creation as well as the immaterial aspects. Consequently, everything we do in the world is spiritual.

The book of Proverbs teaches us how to take dominion, how to distinguish Lady Wisdom from Harlot Folly, to avoid the gang of ne'er-do-wells and listen to your father and mother, learning how to speak, how to do business, handle wealth, and more. In other words, Proverbs is not any less "spiritual" or "theological" than the rest of the Scriptures. (I would add that Leviticus and Romans are not any less practical than Proverbs, but that is another subject for another time.)

Proverbs is useful in its practicality, but we may be tempted to think that Proverbs is simple. At one level it is. Sometimes the meanings of the analogies are obvious. "Where there are no oxen, the manger is clean, but abundant crops come by the strength of the ox" (Prov 14:4). Simple enough. If you are a farmer, having oxen will produce its own work because you will have dirty stalls. If your greatest desire is clean stalls, oxen will be a problem. But if you want your farm to be as productive as it can be, you will need to make the trade-off between having dirty stalls and more produce.

This was true in agriculture in the past. But how does this relate to other areas of life? Children come with challenges, but is the trade-off worth it? Where are other areas of life that we must make trade-offs? Quite frankly? Everywhere. You cannot have clean stalls *and* a highly productive farm. That is not how life works. You cannot have a good economy and lockdowns. You cannot have a great, healthy family and not spend time together.You cannot have a socialistic utopia and a productive, wealthy society. Proverbs 14:4 is one of the easiest proverbs, but even it requires digging below the surface of the object to the analogy, meditating on all the relationships involved.

Proverbs also are, as Solomon says, *enigmas* ("saying" in ESV) and "riddles" (or "dark sayings"). They are mysterious, sayings that must be figured out. There is more to them than meets the eye. What's more, to really understand them, the proverbs must be *applied*. This is the challenge and call of wisdom. With all its surface-level practicality, Proverbs calls for the work of meditation, contemplation, thinking, and action.

The Author

Solomon, son of David, king of Israel, is the author of Proverbs, but it is clear from Proverbs itself that not every proverb is written by Solomon. For example, he collected "the sayings of the wise," or the "words of the wise," according to Proverbs 22:17 and Proverbs 24:23. This is exactly what you would expect a wise man to do: Collect wisdom from other wise people, to learn from others.

Agur, son of Jakeh, writes what is recorded in Proverbs 30. King Lemuel writes Proverbs 31. Some people have tried to make these pseudonyms for Solomon, but this need not be the case. The Psalms are attributed to David, but David collected Psalms from Moses, and Asaph also wrote many Psalms. The book of Proverbs was written under the supervision of Solomon. They are all Solomon-approved.

Why Proverbs?

Why did Solomon write the book of Proverbs? What need did he see?

Proverbs is a catechism for princes, kings-in-waiting, young men who need to be trained in how to deal with the realities of the world when they reach a certain stage of maturity.

The works of wisdom literature, as a whole, came at a time in Israel's history in which the people were moving from childhood to young adulthood. In biblical categories, they are moving from a priestly stage to a kingly stage.[1] In the priestly stage, everything was spelled out for them. There were clear-cut rules in black and white, such as what to do when a lizard fell in your pot or how you needed to build your home to keep people from falling off of your roof. As history progressed and they matured into a kingdom, situations changed. They never left the priestly stage completely behind. The fear of Yahweh, basic allegiance to the worship of God, is fundamental and will remain. Just as a writer never leaves the fundamentals of the alphabet or a composer never leaves the fundamentals of musical notes, so Israel never *left* the priestly aspect of their existence.

However, they were supposed to mature. And with maturity comes new challenges for which there cannot be rules for everything. Rooted in the fundamentals, they must arrange letters into new and more complex words and concepts and the musical notes into more glorious music. They must be able to respond to the complexities of life for which there are no hard-and-fast rules and make something good, true, beautiful, and productive out of it.

---

1. For a more extended discussion of the stages of priest, king, and prophet, see Jeffrey Meyers, *A Table In The Mist* (Monroe, LA: Athanasius Press, 2006), 28-30. For an even more extended discussion, see James B. Jordan, *From Bread To Wine: Creation, Worship, and Christian Maturity* (West Monroe, LA: Theopolis Books, 2019), 11-22.

Solomon, the wise king, composed Proverbs as a catechism for princes, to train them in the way of wisdom. Throughout Proverbs, especially in the first section, we notice that Solomon speaks directly to his son or his sons. Right after an introductory salvo, Solomon declares, "Hear, my son, your father's instruction" (Prov 1:8). Who is his son?

The son in question need not be some now-unknown person, or a general term for any reader or listener. Solomon actually had a son who would succeed him as king: Rehoboam. There is something of an autobiographical statement in Proverbs 4. Solomon recounts receiving wisdom from his father, David, whom he names in the title. Solomon is passing on that wisdom in addition to what he has acquired.

After Solomon died, Rehoboam took the throne. Learning from history, we understand that teaching wisdom is not a panacea for fools, which Solomon tells us throughout Proverbs:

"Why should a fool have money in his hand to buy wisdom when he has no sense?" (Prov 17:6).

"Like a lame man's legs, which hang useless, is a proverb in the mouth of fools" (Prov 26:7).

"Crush a fool in a mortar with a pestle along with crushed grain, yet his folly will not depart from him" (Prov 27:22).

Wisdom is useless for a man given over to his foolishness because his foolishness goes to the bone, the deepest part of his being. You can be one of the wisest men to ever live and still have a fool for a son.

While the book of Proverbs is, I believe, first and foremost written to Solomon's sons, and particularly Rehoboam, it is written to all sons—young, maturing men. Our curiosity should be piqued when he addresses his son throughout but never his daughters. (Solomon's Song of Songs might be his address to the daughters.) Some might say, "Well, this is inclusive language, and the son also represents the daughters." I do not think so. Solomon addresses women indirectly in Proverbs. There is much for women to learn and much to learn about women in Proverbs, but it is principally focused on the young *man*.

Why?

Bruce Waltke offers this explanation: "Instead of mentioning his daughter, the father singles out his son because the male offspring is expected to assume the leadership in defining the family's identity and values (Prov 4:3-4; see also Numbers 30)."[2] The man is principally responsible for the mission of ruling over the creation. Therefore, the mission of dominion is chiefly his responsibility. He needs wisdom to complete this mission, so Solomon directs his instruction in wisdom to his son.

The woman has responsibility as well, but it is not the same as the man. The woman is highly praised and exalted.

---

2. Bruce Waltke, *New International Commentary on the Old Testament: Proverbs*, Vol. 1 (Grand Rapids, MI: William B. Eerdmans Publishing Company, 2004), 117.

She is of great worth and embodiment of wisdom that he needs as his companion (Proverbs 31). But she is all these things as she fulfills her responsibility as a woman, which is not the same as the man. The greater burden is on the man. He is responsible for the total mission for the world, which includes being responsible for the woman.

Her responsibilities are related to *his* mission, as it is with Christ and the church. The woman is integral in fulfilling this mission. Wisdom is embodied as a woman. The man cannot complete his mission without wisdom. The man cannot complete his mission without the woman. This is reflective of the opening chapters of Genesis: The man needs the woman to complete his mission. Wisdom is the indispensable, invaluable helper.

Wisdom is skill in understanding relationships, how things and people fit together to make what is good, true, beautiful, and productive. But wisdom, being personal, is embodied in the woman, Lady Wisdom: the woman who has built her house, slaughtered her beasts, mixed her wine, set her table, and calls out to the simple (Prov 9:1-12). She is the woman who, because of her wise productivity, causes her husband to be known in the places of authority in the city as he sits among the elders (Prov 31:23). She, Lady Wisdom, is the glory of the man.

Finding her is not difficult. She is plain to see and hear. But in a fallen world, it will be challenging. Two women are vying for the prince's attention: Lady Wisdom and Harlot Folly. This is different from the situation involving the first man and woman.

In the beginning, God puts man to sleep, and from the man's side he creates the woman and brings her to the man. The Father arranged the marriage for his son, giving him no other choice. That is no longer the case. Man must now choose a wife between two types of women. His decision must be determined in the context of his responsibility and mission.

Man is given a mission to build God's house, to create, rearrange, construct a world that will be a house in which God and man can dwell together. The particulars of Proverbs as well as the overall structure of Proverbs speak to this mission.

While at times the structure of the book of Proverbs seems chaotic and haphazard, there is an overall structure to the book that is really quite clear. There are seven sections in Proverbs (1:1–9:18; 10:1–22:16; 22:17–24:22; 24:23–34; 25:1–29:27; 30:1–33; 31:1–31.)

Why does the book have a seven-fold structure? Because the world has a seven-fold structure. The first week of creation is seven days and therefore the world has a seven-fold structure. The man's mission is to create a new world, as it were, with what God has provided.

As we know from Proverbs 8, Wisdom builds worlds. As image-bearers of God we build or create worlds, large and small. We do so either wisely or unwisely.

Jesus tells us that we build houses on the sand or on the rock (Matt 7:24-27). But the reality is that we are all house-building, world-creating. We make worlds, ordered spaces, according to the way we speak and act, our way of thinking and the decisions we make. We *are* world-builders, constructing everything from our individual lives to homes to societies.

Proverbs begins, interestingly enough, by telling the son the purpose is for him "to understand a proverb and an enigma, the words of the wise and their *dark sayings*." Proverbs begins with darkness and then, methodically, separates light from darkness in the first section (Proverbs 1-9). Proverbs ends with instructions to King Lemuel and praise of Lady Wisdom, king and queen enthroned over creation. Enthronement is a Sabbath theme. God was enthroned over the creation on the original seventh day to enjoy his creation. In man's work-rest pattern, we are called to enter into his Sabbath rest following the same pattern. The king and queen are enthroned at the end. There is a great deal to sort out in between the first day and the last day.

Much of the book's contents (Proverbs 10-24), though they have some discernible connections and form literary sections, are something of a mix between order and disorder. Even this form is instructive for the son and his mission. This is the world he has been called to subdue. Duane Garrett observes,

> Also the very disorder of a collection of proverbs can serve a didactic purpose; it demonstrates that while reality and truth are not irrational, neither are they fully subject to human attempts at systemization. The proverbs are presented in the seemingly haphazard way we encounter the issues with which they deal.[3]

---

3. Duane A. Garrett, *The New American Commentary: Proverbs, Ecclesiastes, Song of Songs*, Vol. 14 (Nashville, TN: Broadman Press, 1993), 46.

This section of Proverbs is, in a sense, "unarranged." As such, Solomon is teaching his son at least two things about the creation.

First, this is how you will face situations in life. Everything will not be neat and tidy but will hit you in what seems to be a random fashion.

Second, Proverbs 10-24 invites us to arrange the material as part of the larger project. This does not mean the arrangement in Scripture is uninspired or needs to be changed. It is more like all the pieces of a one-thousand-piece puzzle that your father puts before you to put together in a coherent picture, without giving you the box top as a reference. Proverbs 10-24 is like a mosaic made up of smaller, complete pictures. Each proverb can stand on its own, but it also makes a larger picture when put together. Like Wisdom, the master craftsman, who takes the unformed and unfilled and arranges it into an ordered, beautiful creation, we are invited to do the same with this literary section as training for making sense of the world and arranging it.

Man cannot complete this task without Wisdom. He needs the woman. He needs a helper. But his wisdom begins by choosing the right woman. One woman will help him with his mission. One will destroy him and his mission. He must learn to discern the difference between the two.

This will be a life-long task. What we learn from Solomon's introduction is that you never graduate from the school of wisdom. Though he is writing Proverbs to his son at a particular time, the proverbs will be useful throughout life. Proverbs 1:4 says that Solomon's objective is to "give prudence to the simple, purposive knowledge to the youth—Let the wise hear and increase in learning, and the one who understands obtain guidance." Proverbs is for young men, but it is also for wise, older men. We never stop learning wisdom. Because we will never be all-wise, we will always be growing in wisdom, and Proverbs is useful for young and old alike.

Solomon wants his son to *know wisdom* (Prov 1:2-6). Wisdom is about relationships, more particularly about being skillful in relationships, whether that be in an artistic fashion or in executing justice (i.e., right relationships between humans).

Though we will never be all-wise as God is, God shares his wisdom with us. He does not make it easy. As we learn in Proverbs 25:2, it is the glory of God to conceal a matter, and it is the glory of kings to search out a matter. God wants us to search for wisdom. Though the task is difficult, it is not impossible. Indeed, the purpose of Proverbs is *to know wisdom.* Solomon desires that his son have *knowledge* of wisdom.

Knowledge, wisdom, and understanding form something of a trinity throughout Proverbs. Like the Trinity itself, they can be distinguished but not separated. Each has a particular emphasis that, quite frankly, can be difficult to express.

"To know" or "knowledge" is more than having an intellectual comprehension (although it is not less than that). Facts are indispensable to knowledge, but not the totality of knowledge. Knowledge is relational. Knowledge is *a right relationship with reality that positions you to be fruitful or productive.* Knowledge recognizes the "grain of reality" and lines itself up with it so as to be productive.

When the Bible describes the relationship between husband and wife that results in conception, it uses the verb "to know." Genesis 4:1 says, "Adam knew his wife Eve and she conceived and bore Cain." The conception of Cain, at minimum, required a comprehension of facts. For example, Adam had to understand that Eve was a woman as well as her differences from him and how the two of them fit together. But Adam's knowing of Eve was more than an intellectual exercise. It was a relationship with another part of God's creation that resulted in fulfilling a God-given purpose—to be fruitful and multiply.

"To know wisdom" is to discern reality (the way God created and sustains the world), love it, commit oneself to it so as to be fruitful.

In Proverbs 1:4, where most have the translation, "knowledge and discretion," I think it should probably be translated "purposive knowledge." That is, knowledge which has such a relationship with reality that it can make workable plans that will be fruitful, fulfilling your created purpose. Knowledge submits to reality.

True knowledge, however, is not superficial. We learn throughout Proverbs that wisdom is a matter of heart commitment. Knowing wisdom is internalizing reality as God has declared it so that it controls thoughts and desires. It is submitting to God's reality, which *is* reality. You do not merely intellectually comprehend the fact that you are a male or female, but you accept that fact and live with the way God created you so as to fulfill your God-given purpose. This is the knowledge Proverbs calls us to have.

With wisdom, and inseparable from it, is *discipline*. The ESV consistently translates the word for "discipline" as "instruction" in Proverbs, but "discipline" is a better word that more accurately describes the point of Solomon's teaching.

The word translated "discipline" assumes a correction of waywardness, keeping your thoughts, desires, and actions in line with the way of wisdom. Discipline can come from without or be self-imposed, self-discipline.

Yahweh disciplines sons he loves, and we are not to despise that discipline (Prov 3:11-12). Young children are disciplined by their parents to drive foolishness from their hearts (Prov 22:15; 23:13-14). But the purpose of all discipline is to learn how to resist evil ourselves—without being beaten, and to learn self-discipline or self-control, controlling your impulses. It is to develop integrity, or moral strength.

Solomon wants his son to know discipline, to have a proper relationship to discipline, to heed the warnings and turn from the way of destruction. There is no wisdom without discipline.

He further explains in Proverbs 1:3 that discipline in wise dealing will have three characteristics: righteousness, justice, and equity. Prudence, or wisdom, will seek to shape people and the world according to these three characteristics.

Righteousness is conformity to the right standard. Justice is the proper reconciliation of relationships that brings about peace. Equity is fairness, leveling out things between people in a proper fashion. If a son disciplines his wayward desires, bringing them under his rule, and is not swayed by things like bribes or the seduction of women, he will be able to help build a world of peace, whether that be in his own home, the church, a business, or a nation.

Discipline is an indispensable key to wisdom.

Solomon wants his son to, literally rendered, "understand words of understanding." There are a couple of different words translated "understanding" throughout Proverbs. The word used in the book's introduction has the emphasis on discernment. It could be translated, in poor English, "to insight words of insight." The word involves seeing a contrast between ways of living or between women, and to discern what the end of choices will be. What does following this path look like several years down the road? What does instant gratification with this woman look like compared to patiently waiting for my lady wisdom and being satisfied with the wife of my youth? Solomon wants his son to have discernment regarding the consequence of his choices *so that* he can avoid destruction in the future and enjoy the life God created for him.

Another theme woven throughout the book and its introduction is *personal responsibility*. Solomon is teaching wisdom, but he cannot force you to learn it. Solomon shows his sons two ways, describing the horrors of one way of living and the beauties of the other, but he cannot make his sons choose the right way.

There comes a point in parenting, or in any other leadership position, when you must recognize your personal limitations, your lack of control over people and be content with being faithful in presenting the alternatives to them. After doing that, it is the choice of the listener as to whether or not he wants to live in the way of the wise or the way of the fool.

Personal responsibility directs the warp and woof of the book of Proverbs. You make choices. Regardless of the influences in your life, you make the choice to do this or that. The responsibility for those choices is yours.

If you choose, for example, to go with the gang instead of listening to your father and mother, and everything comes crashing down around you in your stubborn disobedience, wisdom will laugh at you when you suffer for your choice (Prov 1:20ff.). If you despise discipline and choose the way of death, you will die. If you are slothful, you will be unproductive and suffer for it. If you bed down with Harlot Folly, she will put you in the grave with all her other victims.

The unrepentant fool will rage against the Lord for how his life turned out. "When a man's folly brings his way to ruin, his heart rages against Yahweh" (Prov 19:3). He will blame God and everyone but himself and his choices. It was his parents, his church family, the government, systemic racism—something or someone, just not him. He refuses to take any personal responsibility.

When the wise is rebuked for his folly, he repents, learns, and gets back on the path. He takes responsibility for his choices. If you choose the way of life, the way of wisdom, you will live. If you accept discipline and are patient, there will be great reward. If you are diligent, you will be fruitful.

Wisdom is calling. What is your answer?

Proverbs 1:7

The fear of Yahweh is the beginning of knowledge;
fools despise wisdom and instruction.

CHAPTER 4

The Fear of the Lord

The fear of the Lord is fundamental and pervasive to righteous living, but it is widely misunderstood. Throughout Scripture, we are encouraged and commanded on numerous occasions to fear God. Ecclesiastes 12:13 says that fearing God and keeping his commandments is the whole duty of man. But we read in 1 John 4:18, "There is no fear in love, but perfect love casts out fear." God and his messengers repeatedly instruct us, "Fear not." How do we resolve this apparent contradiction?

Exodus 20 represents all these senses in one passage:

> Now when all the people saw the thunder and the flashes of lightning and the sound of the trumpet and the mountain smoking, the people *trembled,* and they stood far off and said to Mo-

ses, "You speak to us, and we will listen; but do not let God speak to us, lest we die." Moses said to the people, "***Do not fear***, for God has come to test you, ***that the fear of him may be before you, that you may not sin***" (Exod 20:18-20).

"Do not fear" because God has come to test you "that the *fear of him* may be before you." Do not fear because God wants you to fear. Any honest hearer or reader is confused. So, are we to fear or are we not to fear? Yes. Just as with anything else in Scripture, or in any other literature for that matter, we must understand the different senses and contexts of a word or idea.

This is the foundational statement for the book of Proverbs: "The fear of Yahweh is the beginning of knowledge; fools despise wisdom and instruction." The fear of Yahweh is *the* fundamental quality that separates the wise and the fool. Without the fear of Yahweh, you cannot begin to find the way of wisdom.

When Solomon says the fear of Yahweh is the *beginning* of knowledge, he is *not* saying the fear of Yahweh is like the starting line in a race. Rather, the *beginning* is the first and controlling principle. "What the alphabet is to reading, notes to reading music, and numerals to mathematics, the fear of the Lord is to attaining the revealed knowledge of this book."[1] The fear of Yahweh is the quality on which you build the rest of your life, not a beginning stage that is left behind.

---

1. Waltke, Vol. 1, 181.

What is the fear of Yahweh, or the fear of the Lord? To answer that question, we must understand fear itself.

What is Fear?

Everyone knows what fear is, right? Whether a child or adult, we have each experienced fear.

When afraid, our minds race. Our palms get sweaty. There is a sudden rush of adrenaline when you see that the other car is not going to stop at the red light, and you are moving through the intersection. Your life flashes before your eyes and the thought of protecting the children is all you can think about.

Yes, this and many other situations are the experience of fear, so we think we understand it. But just as with all of Proverbs—indeed, all of Scripture!—we must meditate on what has been said so that we can understand our experience of fear.

Fear is when *our disposition is controlled by something or someone outside of us, whether real or perceived, drawing us closer to what/who we love and repelling us from what/who threatens the beloved.*

Fear is frequently associated with our emotions, our fight or flight response. Our adrenaline spikes and we are overwhelmed with a sense of dreadful excitement and moved to action, whether it is physical confrontation with another person, animal, or circumstance, or even our internal wrestling, our anxiety. Our fears move us to action, even if it is limited to the action of our minds.

Our emotional response of fear is where our deep, abiding fears express themselves, but what they are expressing runs much deeper than our emotions. Fear always resides in our hearts, controlling our actions for good or ill. As Michael Reeves says in his book, *Rejoice and Tremble*, "...fear of any sort is something that runs deeper than behavior: it is something in the very grain of the heart that *drives* behavior."[2] Fear is a constitutional part of being human. One reason for this is that we are created in the image of fear himself. (I will explain that in a moment.) People and circumstances *reveal* our fears, and our emotions give expression to those fears. Fear, however, is always there, a part of who we are.

Fear controls our disposition

I use the word *disposition* because this word speaks about how our whole person is oriented toward something or someone. Our minds, wills, emotions, and actions are inclined a certain way. Whether sinful or righteous, fear controls our disposition.

We are overwhelmed with a sense of weakness or lack of control. We are subject to influences beyond us. If something is perceived as a threat, we are anxious and driven away. If something is perceived as friendly or lovely, we may be full of awe and drawn near. There may still be danger in either case. We know this thing or person is dangerous in some way, but the danger of what is loved is intriguing, inspiring exploration, devotion, and a desire for intimacy.

---

2. Michael Reeves, *Rejoice and Tremble: The Surprising Good News of the Fear of the Lord* (Wheaton, IL: Crossway, 2021), 110.

Most of us, if not all of us, are rightly afraid of poisonous snakes. I grew up in the country, hunting and fishing, frequently encountering cottonmouth moccasins as well as copperheads. Whenever I saw them, whatever else I was doing became secondary. At that point, everything about me was focused on that snake. This is a good fear because snakes can do serious damage. Whenever I encountered one of these snakes, I feared. I was controlled, not just by the snake, but by love for myself, self-preservation, which is a good self-love when kept within godly boundaries. I would either get away from the snake or kill him. (I always preferred the latter if there was a good stick or gun at hand.)

We clearly identify this feeling as fear. This is feeling of fear is normally conjured in our minds when we think of fear. But think about walking in the mountains, or, better yet, into a massive cathedral, beautifully built. (If you have never been to a cathedral or a building like it, stick with the mountains.) These massive structures and artwork are *intimidating*, which is just another form of fear. However, it is not a repulsive fear. The beauty, while being overwhelming and intimidating, is magnetic, drawing you into itself. In one sense, you want to be consumed by it, and get lost in it. There are times when you can be so overwhelmed in a situation like this that you tremble in pleasurable agony.

These two types of fear meet in our relationships, when there is an attraction between a man and a woman. The other one is appealing, drawing us closer. We are overwhelmed, excited, with sweaty palms, desiring to be closer, but we can, at the same time, be afraid of rejection. We tremble both in joy and fright at the prospects. Fear takes on two forms in one situation. This is because there is a very thin and sometimes even blurred line, between revulsion and pleasure, between being afraid and being joyful.

Fear sharpens and focuses the mind

Whenever your fears express themselves emotionally in fight, flight, or anxiety, your thinking is consumed with the object of fear, sharpening your focus on that one thing.

> Fear also has a tendency to create a groove in our minds: the more we fear something, the more we become engrossed with it and can't let it go.... Whether we are fascinated or repelled by the object of our fear, there are common traits to all our fears: they arise from what we love, they excite the body, and they fixate the mind.[3]

Think about when you are anxious. Anxiety is fear. You have lost control of a person or situation that is threatening you with the loss of something you love. At that point, your desire and aim are to regain control, which you may or may not be able to do. Your mind is consumed with the situation. You are focused, fixated on what went wrong and how to resolve it. This is all you can think about.

The same could be true in being overwhelmed with that which is lovely such as the cathedral mentioned earlier (or a lover, or a piece of music). Everything else is lost for that time. You can't see or hear things around you. Your

---

3. Reeves, *Rejoice*, 28, 29.

mind is consumed, fixated, focused on that which is over-whelming you.

Fear is rooted in love

All this is true because fear is rooted in love. You are afraid because you are threatened in some way with the loss of what is loved. When the beloved is threatened, you run to the beloved and try to protect it, standing against any ene-mies. "Wilhelmus à Brakel explained that 'fear issues forth from love.' That is, we fear *because* we love: we love our-selves and so fear bad things happening to us; we love our families, our friends, our things and so fear losing them."[4]

Fear, as I said, always resides in the human heart be-cause it is a fierce guardian of our deepest loves. Our fears *reveal* our deepest heart loyalties. What do you love? To an-swer that question, you must ask yourself other questions: What do you try to protect? What are you afraid to lose? A spouse? A child? Your possessions? Your status? Your life?

At this point I am not saying that any of those fears are sinful or righteous, but I am saying that fear is rooted in love, and you can know what or who you love most by what you fear.

Is fear righteous or sinful?

Someone might claim we would never have known fear if sin had not been introduced to the world. The first time we read of fear in Scripture is when Adam tells Yahweh that he

---

4. Ibid, 27.

heard the sound of God walking in the Garden and he was afraid and hid himself (Gen 3:10). But, as you know, this is not the only reference to fear.

Remember this truth about sin: Sin cannot create. Sin only perverts, attaching itself to some righteous quality, distorting it. Sin is parasitic, a cancer that takes what is God-made and poisons it. Fear, therefore, was originally a righteous quality. Throughout Scripture it is presented as a righteous quality, as seen in Proverbs 1:7: "The fear of Yahweh is the beginning of knowledge." As I mentioned in earlier, Ecclesiastes 12:13 says fearing God is part and parcel to the whole duty of man. In Isaiah 11:2-3, when the anointing of the Spirit is prophesied for the Messiah, one of the gifts of the Spirit is *the fear of Yahweh*. The messiah's *delight* will be in the fear of Yahweh.

Some might retort, "Well, that is an old creation phenomenon because back then God was mean and scary. Since Christ has come, we don't fear God anymore." As you know, there are many problems with such thinking. The New Testament witness is clear. When Mary sings her song in praise of God in response to Elizabeth, she proclaims that God's mercy is on those who fear him (Luke 1:50). We read in 2 Corinthians 7:1 that because we have the promises of being God's new temple, we are to perfect holiness in the fear of God. Peter plainly commands us to "fear God" in 1 Peter 2:17. Many more New Testament witnesses could be called.

Fear is originally a righteous quality because God is fear. Tucked away in a little exchange between Laban and Jacob in Genesis 31 is a name for God that not many people evoke: "The Fear of Isaac." God reveals himself as fear.

This is true of his revelation through his Word, through the Law. In Psalm 19, the Law of Yahweh is described as "the fear of Yahweh." God's word reveals his character, and his character is fear. You and I, therefore, are made in the image of fear because God is fear.

That does not sound right to our ears. How can God be fear? How can God's name be "Jealous"? But the Bible is clear that God's name is "Jealous" (Exod 34:14). How can that be? We tend only to think of the sinful expressions of both fear and jealousy.

"Fear" is a righteous quality. Because God is perfect love, he is also perfect fear; he is not terrified by any loss, but eternally engrossed in the goodness of one another within the Trinity and repulsed by anything that opposes this relationship. God's disposition is controlled by his love for the good and his hatred for evil. He loves what is lovely and destroys what is evil. He is fiercely protective of his beloved so that he loses nothing he loves.

You and I are created in the image of *this* fear, and it is this fear that is twisted by sin. As mentioned, we tend only to understand fear in a negative light because it is expressed sinfully so many times. But fear is righteous.

So, how do you define righteous fear? Righteous fear is when *my disposition is controlled by the love of what is good and, consequently, when I hate what is evil, trembling with longing at the loveliness of the good and trembling with hatred of what is evil.* Righteous fear is drawn to what is good and repulsed by that which would seek to destroy the beloved good. Righteous fear fights against threats to the beloved. This is why we hear in Proverbs 8:13, "The fear of Yahweh is hatred of evil." And again in Proverbs 16:6, we read, "by the fear of Yahweh one turns away from evil." Righteous fear is controlled by love for good.

On the other hand, sinful fear is when *we are controlled by the love for the wrong thing so we are repelled from that which is good and driven to that which is evil.* You are drawn to that which is evil and seek to protect it. Sinful fear hates God and his commandments, believing that God is a stingy tyrant not interested in doing good for us but wanting to withhold what is good and destroy us. Sinful fear is rooted in unbelief. The Puritan John Flavel wrote:

> If men would but dig to the root of their fears, they would certainly find unbelief there, Matth. viii. 26. Why are ye afraid, O ye of little faith! The less faith, still the more fear: Fear is generated by unbelief, and unbelief strengthened by fear; … and therefore all the skill in the world can never cure us of the disease of fear, till God first cure us of our unbelief; Christ therefore took the right method to rid his disciples of their fear, by rebuking their unbelief.[5]

Sinful fear is unwilling to trust God, seeing him as a threat to what we love. He is the enemy. He does not care about my life, the life of my family, my possessions, etc. He wants me to love *him* more than I love all these things *because he wants to deprive me of these things.* This is the cringing fear of the Israelites at Mount Sinai, the fear that God is there to destroy everything I love, principally *me*.

---

5. "A Practical Treatise on Fear," quoted in Reeves, *Rejoice*, 25.

Now we turn to the principal question:

What is the fear of the Lord?

We know from Scripture there is a proper and improper fear of God. We know from what John says in 1 John 4:18 that "There is no fear in love; but perfect love casts out fear." But what kind of fear is this? John goes on to explain, "…because fear involves punishment. But he who fears has not been made perfect in love."

Such a cringing attitude toward God fears he is only there to torment and punish you. You are not accepted or loved by him. He is there to take away from you everything you love. This is not the fear of God that is commended to us or commanded of us. This is where God says to us, "Fear not!"

Many have said that proper fear of God means respect, reverence, or awe of God. All these are involved in the fear of the Lord, but none of those words captures what the Scriptures mean in describing the "fear of the Lord."

Let's apply our definition of fear: the fear of the Lord is *when our disposition is controlled by our love for God, drawing us closer to him and repelling us from whatever threatens our relationship.* Our greatest fear, the deepest love and loyalty of our hearts, is God himself. Our love for him overwhelms us, consumes us, causes us to tremble with joyful fear, and hates anything that would disappoint him or damage the relationship.

We know God is dangerous. That is part of his overwhelming glory. But we also know he is on our side, so we can stand in awe of his power while still rejoicing with quaking. We certainly are afraid of ever being found to be an enemy of God. The dread of being separated from him and being the object of his wrath are unimaginable.

This fear arises from love and is characteristic of love. The Scriptures make the parallel between the fear of God and love of God, as in Psalm 145:19-20: "He will fulfill the desire of ***those who fear Him***; He also will hear their cry and save them. Yahweh preserves ***all who love Him***, But all the wicked He will destroy." The same parallel is in Deuteronomy 6:4-15 where Moses calls Israel to "love Yahweh their God with all of their heart" (v. 5) and later says, "it is Yahweh your God you shall fear" (v. 15).

Fear of God is a fierce loyalty that controls how we think, speak, desire, and act. The difference between righteous fear of God and sinful fear of God is love: Do you love God above everything else? Do you see God as a tyrant who withholds what you love so that you are driven away from him? That is the fear of punishment of which John speaks. That is the revelation of a deep-seated hatred of God in your heart.

We will battle this inclination throughout our lives. We all have the remnants of corruption that plague our hearts, a hatred of God in his holiness. Love of God drives out this hatred. Our love has not yet been perfected.

Do you see God as a loving Father who protects you from what harm, who wants what is best for you, and who fights for you? Do you long to be in a healthy relationship with him above all else so you are drawn to everything that deepens the intimacy of that relationship and you have a growing hatred of the things that damage that relationship?

Do you dread disappointing him? Does your heart take delight in him?

Interestingly, one of the two common Hebrew words translated fear (Heb *phd)* is used in Isaiah 60:5 to speak of a joyful emotion: "Then you shall see and be radiant; your heart shall thrill (fear) and exult, because the abundance of the sea shall be turned to you, the wealth of the nations shall come to you." The renowned Reformed scholar John Murray comments on this usage: "Apparently the thought is that the heart throbs with pleasure."[6]

Nehemiah 11:1 speaks about delighting to fear God's name. When God does good things, people are overwhelmed with this joyful fear. We hear it in Jeremiah 33:9: "And this city shall be to me a name of joy, a praise and a glory before all the nations of the earth who shall hear of all the good that I do for them. *They shall fear and tremble because of all the good and all the prosperity I provide for it."* The word emphasizes a physical response of being overwhelmed, weak-kneed, trembling, or being staggeringly discomposed.[7] This same word can be used for "bone-melting dread"[8]: "The sinners in Zion are afraid [*phd*]; trembling has seized the godless: 'Who among us can dwell with the consuming fire? Who among us can dwell with everlasting burnings?'" (Isa 33:14) The difference is whether we are drawn closer in fear or repulsed in fear.

---

6. John Murray, *Principles of Conduct: Aspects of Biblical Ethics* (Grand Rapids, MI: William B. Eerdmans Publishing Co., 1957), 232, n. 1.

7. Reeves, *Rejoice*, 57.

8. Ibid.

Some want to draw hard and fast lines between these two types of fear, but sometimes they have many of the same characteristics. And, as sinners, there is still a mixture. Speaking of the words translated "fear," Murray says:

> [One word] is used of the fear of God most frequently and does service for both senses in which we may fear God: (1) the fear of being afraid of God and his punitive judgments; (2) the fear of reverential awe and adoration.... We are not to think that these two meanings are antithetical or incompatible.[9]

Consider your relationship with your earthly father, or, alternatively, imagine having a good relationship with an earthly father. You love your father, sometimes even if he is not all that good. If you had a loving father, you were still scared of him at some point. He was larger than life. If your mother wanted to get you to do something or to stop doing something, threatening you with your father was always an option. You were not scared he would throw you out of the house or even beat you mercilessly. You were afraid of disappointing him, of being the object of displeasure, of making him sad. (There was also the fact that he spanked harder than mom as well.) Dad was fearful, but it was because you loved him so much and hungered for a good relationship with him. To hear dad say, "Good job! I'm proud of you" was—and maybe still is—the highest honor you can have because of your love for him.

---

9. Murray, *Principles of Conduct*, 231, n. 1.

This is healthy fear. This is analogous to the way we fear God in a righteous manner.

The fear of the Lord controls our disposition.

We sense our weakness and our lack of control in his presence. We are overwhelmed. The fear of the Lord controls our minds, wills, emotions, and actions.

The fear of the Lord sharpens and focuses our minds.

Fear draws our focus to the object of our fear, sharpening and fixating our minds. The fear of the Lord fixes our minds upon him.

The fear of the Lord is rooted in love.

We love the Lord and are drawn to his awesome majesty, desire a good, healthy relationship with him, and dread anything that would disrupt the relationship or disappoint our God. We do not dread the possibility that he would throw us out of his house, so to speak, but we dread the thought of doing anything disappointing to him. As Charles Spurgeon said, "Holy fear leads us to dread anything which might cause our Father's displeasure."[10] We love him and loathe that which is his enemy and the enemy to our relationship.

With a better understanding of the fear of the Lord, we can understand Solomon's statement concerning the fear of Yahweh as the beginning of knowledge, or wisdom.

How is the fear of the Lord the beginning of knowledge?

Knowledge is a right relationship with reality that puts you in a position to be productive, to fulfill your God-given

---

10. Quoted in Reeves, *Rejoice*, 102.

purpose. Knowledge is more than just a grasp of the facts, though a grasp of the facts is necessary. It is an acceptance of reality, putting yourself in line with or in submission to reality, and is thus a matter of character.

The fear of the Lord is the fundamental reality that puts you in right relationship with reality and sets you up to be productive, to fulfill your purpose in God's world. You cannot know yourself or the world the way you should without the fear of the Lord. The fear of the Lord is foundational for showing you what is good and evil, the shape of reality, what to avoid and what to pursue. The fear of the Lord is basic to understanding the way of life.

As we would expect, the fear of the Lord is also the beginning of wisdom (Prov 9:10; Psa 111:10). God and his purposes are good. He and he alone knows how the world is supposed to operate and what is the best outcome. If you do not love him and his purposes, submitting to his will, you forsake the foundation of wisdom. You may get some things correct, but you cannot put a world together that is good, true, beautiful, and productive. You are building on shifting sands. The rock upon which to build the house is the fear of the Lord.

The only question left is, do you fear God? Do you fear him more than man? The only way to answer that question faithfully is to determine who controls you. Your love, your fear, will always be revealed in what you do more than in what you say.

Proverbs 30:1-6

The words of Agur son of Jakeh. The oracle.
  The man declares, I am weary, O God;
    I am weary, O God, and worn out.
  Surely I am too stupid to be a man.
    I have not the understanding of a man.
  I have not learned wisdom,
    nor have I knowledge of the Holy One.
  Who has ascended to heaven and come down?
    Who has gathered the wind in his fists?
  Who has wrapped up the waters in a garment?
    Who has established all the ends of the earth?
  What is his name, and what is his son's name?
    Surely you know!
  Every word of God proves true;
    he is a shield to those who take refuge in him.
  Do not add to his words,
    lest he rebuke you and you be found a liar.

CHAPTER 5

Wisdom Revealed

The year was 1991. Susan and I had been married for one year. I was in seminary, and we were invited to go on a short-term mission trip to Tokyo, Japan. We stayed with a lady who spoke no English. Our saving grace was that some of her family members did speak English. One day we had to go to the train station in the heart of Tokyo to meet up with our team. Our hostess, whom we respectfully called Okasan ("mother"), had to drive us there. She pulled up to the train station and used the only two English words she probably knew, "Get out." We did. Trains were going this way and that. Information about the trains was displayed in three different Japanese alphabets—Hiragana, Katakana, and Kanji—in a city that, at that time, was approximately 33 million strong. Not one word of English. We knew what a train was. We recognized other humans. But we had no idea what to do. Eventually, a Japanese man who spoke English saw two desperate, young twenty-something Americans and had mercy on us. If it were not for him giving us directions, Susan and I could be in some Shinto shrine to this day.

In order to function properly in any situation, you need someone at some point to show you the way. Whether it is parents or a local resident at a train station, wisdom must come from outside of you in order to orient you to the world around you. This is true with our existence in God's world as his creatures. We need him to explain to us who we are, why we are here, and where we are going. We need his wisdom.

In our rebellion against him, we refuse his wisdom, and, like the man Agur describes in Proverbs 30:1-4, we cannot find wisdom apart from God.

Frustrating Search for Wisdom

As Agur describes the quest for wisdom, focusing on the frustrations and fruitlessness of a search for wisdom apart from God's revelation, he speaks of his wisdom as divine revelation. In the introduction to his collection of proverbs, Agur identifies his words as a prophetic utterance: "The words/sayings" and "the oracle" (translated as "utterance" by some). In contrast to the search described in the first few verses, Agur relies on divine revelation for his wisdom. This should be the course of action for all men, but, sadly, men go their own way.

The second half of Proverbs 30:1 is variously translated. Some have taken Agur to be a man declaring words to people named Ithiel and Ucal: "The man declared to Ithiel, to Ithiel and to Ucal" (KJV, NKJV). Others, like the ESV, translate Agur's statement as "I am weary, O God; I am weary, O God, and worn out." The last word translated "worn out" could also be translated "but I can prevail."[1] There seems to be some merit in translating Agur's statement as having to do with wearisomeness in the beginning and prevailing in the end. Man's search for wisdom divorced from divine revelation described in Proverbs 30:2-4 is wearisome, frustrating, and fruitless but gives way to triumph in Proverbs 30:5-6 as he discovers wisdom through divine revelation.

The search for wisdom begins apart from divine revelation in Proverbs 30:2-3. No matter how hard he has searched, no matter what methods he employed, at the end of the search this man describes himself as being "too stupid to be a man. I have not the understanding of a man." He does not know what it means to be a man in this world. He does not understand the meaning and purpose of life and how to put his own life in right relationship with everything around him. Who am I? Why am I here? What is the purpose? He has searched for wisdom, but he has done so with no knowledge of the Holy One, God himself.

Proverbs 30:4 is a transitional statement, a leading set of questions, driving the inquirer to the source of wisdom. But we must read them in frustration first. Who has ascended to heaven and come down? To achieve eternal truth about the world and its meaning one would have to go into

---

1. Bruce Waltke, *New International Commentary on the Old Testament: Proverbs*, Vol. 2 (Grand Rapids, MI: William B. Eerdmans Publishing Company, 2004), 468.

heaven and bring it back down to earth. No man has done this. No man has made this journey and, consequently, no man can be the source of wisdom. Indeed, man has little if any control over anything.

In a series of three questions, Agur shows the relative powerlessness of man and, therefore, his inability to put the world together wisely. "Who has gathered the wind in his fists? Who has wrapped up the waters in a garment? Who has established all the ends of the earth?" These questions are somewhat reminiscent of Yahweh's speech with Job at the end of his book. There is no man who has the power over the creation to this extent. There is no man, who has the wisdom to put all of this together. So, the final question of frustration—that also leads to the correct answer!—is, "What is his name, and what is his son's name? Surely you know!"

We search in vain through the world for a man who is the source of wisdom. Not even Agur who writes these wise words claims to be *the* source of wisdom. The search for wisdom in man himself and his resources is a futile search. Agur alludes to why this is: man's limitations. As Bruce Waltke concludes,

> To know the skill of living, which entails making wise decisions, one must know everything. In Proverbs old age has superiority over youth because the aged have seen and experienced more than the young. Gray hair is their crown and

splendor (20:29). But no human being sees and knows everything.[2]

To truly know something or someone you have to know everything comprehensively, every consequence to every thought, word, and deed, every relationship of one thing to everything else, *and* you must know why or the purpose for all of these things. To know the basics of something's design, or how it works is not true knowledge. You must know its purpose. Its purpose is a part of knowing it.

One can "know" what a hammer looks like and even design a perfect hammer based upon observation. But if he does not know the purpose of the hammer and seeks to use the hammer to cut a piece of wood, his knowledge is not true knowledge and certainly not wisdom. The same is true for human relationships. People can know how human bodies work, what they are made of, how they work in relationship with one another both physically and psychologically, but if they do not understand the purpose, the end, of human relationships, they do not have true knowledge even if they have certain facts correct.

C. S. Lewis illustrates this principle well in *The Voyage of the Dawn Treader* and that prickly young rationalist, Eustace Scrubb. The crew of the *Dawn Treader* came to the island of a retired star, Ramandu. After some exchange with the star, Eustace says, "In our world ... a star is a huge ball of flaming gas." Ramandu responded, "Even in your world, my son, that is not what a star is but only what is made of."[3]

---

2. Waltke, Vol. 2, 79.

3. C. S. Lewis, *The Chronicles of Narnia: The Voyage of the Dawn*

Knowing what something is made of is not genuinely *knowing* something. There is quite a bit more to knowing. No man has this kind of knowledge, namely, to know the purpose of every material thing and every action and reaction in the world. In order to have any knowledge you must have all knowledge, or you must know someone who has all knowledge, which is precisely the point to which Agur is leading the reader.

Before we move on to Agur's answer for the discovery of wisdom, we should understand how we ourselves have witnessed and been affected by man's futile search for wisdom. This is not some ethereal subject that is a playground for philosophers in ivory towers of the academy. This frustrating quest for wisdom has a great deal to do with our history as a country and, consequently, where we are today as a society.

Beginning in the seventeenth century, the era of the Enlightenment began. They called it the Enlightenment because they were contrasting it with the period they called "the Dark Ages" that they believed had dominated the last one thousand years or so. The Enlightenment was the "dawn" of human reason. It was the Age of Reason. The so-called Dark Ages were dominated by the church and the superstitions of revelation, or so the philosophers said. A subjection to the church held back progress in the science and the arts and led to wars throughout Europe, or so they said.

The Enlightenment way of thinking took hold around the time of the Thirty Years War in Europe (1618-1648).

Treader (New York: HarperCollins Publishers, 1982), 522.

Voltaire, the father of the Enlightenment, and his heirs sought to free science, the arts, and the nations from war by exalting human reason above divine revelation, privatizing religion. Even the word "religion" has come to mean something different than what it meant historically.[4]

Religion was seen as irrational. It was better to establish public institutions on universal human reason rather than any claims of divine revelation. Revelation cannot be proven by human reason.

John Locke, one of the principal minds that helped shape our country's beliefs, argued that

> Faith is assent to knowledge that is derived from revelation rather than from reason. Therefore, its knowledge, although highly probable, is never certain. Reason and judgment must be used in order to measure the degree of probability of what we are asked to believe by faith.[5]

In 1990, the conservative columnist George Will summarized the philosophy of the Enlightenment and its place in the founding of our country in his article, "Conduct, Coercion, Belief."

---

4. For an extended treatment of how Enlightenment thinkers invented the modern concept of "religion," see William T. Cavanaugh, *The Myth of Religious Violence* (Oxford: Oxford University Press, 2009), 57-122. As the title suggests, Cavanaugh debunks the myth of the "religious wars."

5. Justo Gonzales, *The Story of Christianity* (New York, HarperCollins Publishers, 199), vol 2, 189.

Hence religion is to be perfectly free as long as it is perfectly private—mere belief—but it must bend to the political will (law) as regards conduct. Thus Jefferson held that "operations of the mind" are not subject to legal coercion, but that "acts of the body" are. Mere belief, said Jefferson, in one god or 20, neither picks one's pockets nor breaks one's legs.

Jefferson's distinction rests on Locke's principle (Jefferson considered Locke one of the three greatest men who ever lived) that religion can be useful or can be disruptive, but its truth cannot be established by reason. Hence Americans would not "establish" religion. Rather, by guaranteeing free exercise of religions, they would make religions private and subordinate.[6]

Man's reason, unmoored from revelation, would result in a never-ending progress of peace and prosperity, or so the philosophers promised.

When applied consistently, the results of the Enlightenment have been disastrous. The Age of Reason, or the Enlightenment era, ended with its greatest expression in the French Revolution, quite a bloody affair. From then to now, much of the Western world has followed Enlightenment thinking—and had nothing but wars. There have

---

6. George Will, "Conduct, Coercion, Belief," *The Washington Post*, 1990, https://www.washingtonpost.com/archive/opinions/1990/04/22/conduct-coercion-belief/b3612cd6-d75a-4fc0-8242-c676927d2020/

been great advancements in technology from that time to now, to be sure, but because societies as a whole do not have wisdom, we do not know the purpose of things, we destroy ourselves with our own advances.

Disconnected from divine revelation, man does not understand his purpose. Consequently, his own reason becomes his governing authority. How do I put my life together? What is my meaning and purpose? How do we live together as a society? Each man begins to do what is right in his own eyes. People become disoriented as they are disconnected from reality.

We are living in the wake of Enlightenment rationalism and its inevitable consequence.

The knowledge-brokers in the old Enlightenment world, most recently called Modernism, used their knowledge to create societal structures to control people. Grand stories of "progress," "prosperity," and "peace," worked themselves out in a way that people believed themselves to simply be cogs in a machine while certain people controlled their lives.

The postmodern world rebelled: The structures built to control people had to be destroyed. Each person must be free to determine who he is without structures or strictures controlling him. Thus, attempts at peace are viewed as attempts to control another person. Suspicion becomes society's default disposition. Everyone else, or every group, is perceived as a potential oppressor, seeking to keep me, or us, from determining who we want to be.

We have reasoned apart from divine revelation and been bequeathed gender fluidity, the race wars, and many other problems. We look at Western Civilization right now and we see Agur's description of the frustrating, fruitless search for wisdom apart from divine revelation come to life. We are a confused and anxious culture, not having a clue as to why the solutions that we keep doubling down on are tearing us to pieces. Man's reason has won the ground but destroyed itself in the process.

If the search were to end there, we would certainly be despondent. But Agur brings us relief as he leads us to *the* source of wisdom.

Finding Wisdom Through Revelation

In Proverbs 30:4, Agur is leading us somewhere. What man is there who has done all the things in Agur's questions? What is his name, and what is his son's name? There was no man on earth at that time or even who lived before who could be the answer to his question. Agur wants the frustrated man to see that it is only Yahweh himself who is the answer to these questions and is, therefore, the source of wisdom.

"What is his son's name? Surely you know!" His son's name is Israel. When God called Pharaoh to free Israel, he called Israel his firstborn son (Exod 4:22, 23). Why would Agur direct us to Israel? Because it was through Israel that Yahweh revealed himself. To them, Paul says, were given the oracles of God (Rom 3:2; 9:1-5). Yahweh gave them his instruction, his law, described in Psalm 19:

> The law of Yahweh *is* perfect, converting the soul;
> The testimony of Yahweh *is* sure, making wise the
> simple; The statutes of Yahweh *are* right, rejoic-

ing the heart; The commandment of Yahweh *is* pure, enlightening the eyes; The fear of Yahweh *is* clean, enduring forever; The judgments of Yahweh *are* true *and* righteous altogether.

Yahweh's son, Israel, eventually was represented in Israel's king, David as well as his son, Solomon (2 Sam 7:14). This was the son who would build God's house, which means in part that he would be wise, knowing how to put God's world together because he relied upon what God revealed. The first expression of this son was Solomon, the wise king, who gave us Proverbs, Ecclesiastes, and Song of Solomon as well as the great Temple.

Later, there arose David's greater son, Yahweh's son, Jesus, who is the revelation of the wisdom of God, who is building God's cosmic house, arranging the world under his lordship. In him is revealed how the world works. In him we know reality.

Agur drives us to Proverbs 30:5, telling us what we need in order to be saved from destruction, what we need to have true wisdom, is the word of God. We need divine revelation. But why? Why do we need God to reveal himself and his purposes? Why are we frustrated in our search for wisdom apart from revelation?

We need revelation *because of our created design*. We are created in relationship with God who speaks to us. Even before sin entered the world, revelation was needed. In Genesis 1, God revealed to man the source of his food as well as his mission in the world. In Genesis 2, God spoke to the man, giving him a clear prohibition to stay away from the Tree of the Knowledge of Good and Evil. All this assumes man did not know these things apart from revelation. God had to tell him how to live in relation to him and the world around him.

Human reason has never been independent from God. We need revelation because we are not God. He is the Creator and we are the creatures. We are not God and, therefore, do not know everything.

Human reason, to be sure, is not always untrustworthy. The ability to reason is a God-given ability that reflects the God in whose image we are made. God calls us to make judgments, even from our most immature states, and for that we need reason. John Frame defines *reason* as "our ability to judge consistency and logical validity. It enables us to see whether two statements are logically consistent or inconsistent and when an argument is valid or invalid."[7]

Reason is a God-given human faculty. But like any other human faculty, it can be twisted and used in rebellion against God. Whenever this happens, our reason becomes unreasonable.

Reason needs reference points, origins (presuppositions), a frame or framework from which to work and in which to make sense of information. Reason *always* has a framework from which it works. Reason cannot operate independently of everything. This would be like having a judge issue rulings without any standards. There is always some reference point, or "final authority," the premise that controls all other premises.

---

7. John M. Frame, *The Doctrine of the Word of God* (New Jersey: Presbyterian & Reformed Publishing, 2010), 22.

Let's think about this in the context of American football. Imagine you are from another planet, and you have never seen American football. There are some things that look orderly about it, but why do they call it football when they are carrying the ball in their hands or throwing it with their hands, and not their feet? What are these marks on the grass? Why are they chasing one another around? Why do they stop chasing the guy with the ball when he reaches the end of the markings?

Understanding and reasoning through the actions of all that happens on the field requires revelation, that the rules of the game be explained to you. Within that framework, you can reason why the linemen do what they do, why the quarterback does what he does, etc. Those who *know* the game, its purpose and its rules, reason from those things to yell at the referees when they make a terrible call or cheer when the team performs well. Without a reference point or a framework, you have no idea why the team is doing what it is doing or why the fans are reacting the way they are.

We are created and placed in a world designed by God for a specific purpose. As creatures, even without sin, we need the framework, the reference points, the interpretation of creation by God himself. The need for revelation is not an inherent deficiency in man out of which we should grow. This is our creatureliness. Because we are not God, we are different from him, and he must tell us who he is, how we relate to him, and how we are to live in his world.

He does this by speaking to us and telling us who he is. He acts in history, showing us his character and glory. His creation has his image stamped all over it. His acts of deliverance for his people throughout the years shows us his character and power. We are made in his image and, therefore, he reveals himself in our persons so we can know God to some degree by knowing ourselves.

In a world without sin, this revelation in all these areas would have been the framework in which we would have reasoned about everything. Our reason would have been governed by God's revelation of himself and his ways at every point. As we matured, our knowledge and abilities to reason would have matured as well, but they would have always been grounded in what God had revealed about himself and his purpose for us and all of creation.

Not only does our creatureliness require revelation, but we need revelation *because of sin*. Sin has distorted our thinking as we know from Romans 1. What if you have the wrong reference point? You have not lost your ability to reason, but your reasoning is distorted.

Let's return to the American football game and say that you impose the rules and framework of football—or soccer!—on American football. (The two sports do share the same name, after all.) If you are a fan, you are yelling at everyone all the time because the field is laid out all wrong, the men are using their hands, and the ball is shaped funny. If you are playing the game with a number of people who are playing with the rules of American football, they are wondering why you are trying to kick the ball all the time, or why you don't have a helmet on, and why you keep complaining there is no net. Your reasoning ability is not lost. You are just using a different framework altogether. You need to get sorted out and get on the same page. Your reference points, your framework, needs to change.

While on the field, you can clearly see the shape of the ball, the fact that you are playing on grass, the pads worn by the men, the way they carry and throw the ball, etc. You would have some *knowledge*, some connection with reality. You have observed that if you are carrying the ball and you get in the way of one of those really big guys, you will get hit hard for some reason. You have seen it happen again and again. You do not know why, but they do. So, you know to avoid them because you know that you do not want to get hurt.

You have no idea why they are hitting you, but you know you do not like being hit. You know it is smarter to avoid them than to stand in their way.

You may not understand the purpose of this game, but you know that getting hit by these really big guys is reality. When you are carrying the ball and avoiding the big uglies, you may, like Forrest Gump, run so fast that people start cheering for you because you reached a certain part of the field. Partial knowledge can be productive—doing well in the game—even when you do not understand why.

So it is with people who deny God's revelation, his framework, the ultimate reference point for reality. They are running around here hating the rules of the game, thinking they should be playing a different game and trying to play a different game, but they recognize the realities of what is actually going on even if they do not understand it or hate it. They know that 2 + 2 = 4 even though they cannot tell you why. They want to believe the world we live in is a random banging together of atoms with no rhyme or reason that somehow turned out to be orderly and produced their ability to reason. For them, 2 + 2 = 4 in the rules of their game does not make sense because that is not random, but they accept it and work with it, building roads, bridges, cars, and houses recognizing this is just the way things are whether they like the one who invented the game or not. They can gain insight into the human body and psyche from watching how the game is played in individuals, societies, and throughout history.

Their reasoning is still working and can connect some dots that make sense to some degree. However, because they are not working within the framework of the rules of the game, their knowledge is incomplete and distorted. Consequently, it always leads to wrong conclusions and perverted purposes, even while they mess up and do some good things along the way.

The Scriptures are God's revelation of the game. He defines the players, the rules, and the purpose. If you are to have wisdom, you must rely on God's revelation through the Scriptures. This is your reference point, your framework, for understanding everything. As Cornelius VanTil said in his book, *Christian Apologetics*, "The Bible is thought of as authoritative on everything of which it speaks. Moreover, it speaks of everything."[8] This does not mean the Bible gives comprehensive knowledge of the anatomy of a flower or how to perform surgery. Biblical knowledge does not preclude learning things from laboratory experiments.

This view of Scripture, therefore, involves the idea that there is nothing in this universe on which

---

8. Cornelius VanTil, *Christian Apologetics* (Phillipsburg, NJ: Presbyterian and Reformed Publishing Co., 1976), 2.

human beings can have full and true information unless they take the Bible into account. We do not mean, of course, that one must go to the Bible rather than to the laboratory if one wishes to study the anatomy of the snake. But if one goes only to the laboratory and not also the Bible one will not have a full or even true interpretation of the snake.[9]

You may learn what a snake is made of, but you will not know what a snake is (to riff off of Ramandu).

Knowing something, knowing anything, requires knowing its purpose. Only God reveals the true purpose of all things. Solomon established this earlier in Proverbs, telling us, for instance, in Proverbs 2:6, "For Yahweh gives wisdom; From His mouth *come* knowledge and understanding." The fear of Yahweh is the beginning of knowledge (1:7) and wisdom (9:10). The fear of Yahweh is, in part, the revelation of himself.

Agur also points us to this truth when he says, "Every word of God proves trustworthy." His word has been put to the test and found trustworthy. God's revelation of himself makes sense of life, telling us who we are, why we do what we do, our purpose, etc. He has fully and finally revealed the truth of his word through the resurrection of his Son, Wisdom incarnate, establishing the truth of his revelation. You may reject his revelation to your own peril.

You begin your reasoning and live according to his word for life itself. "He is a shield to those who take refuge

---

9. Ibid.

in him." His revelation is the way to life. It is the way of life. His revelation is sufficient, Agur says, as he warns us not to add to his words lest he rebuke us and we be found liars. God's word does not need improvement or embellishment.

We do not need to be ashamed of the Scriptures because the academicians laugh at its claims of creation and history, or because rationalists tell us miracles cannot happen, or because new moralists tell us its ethics are outdated, or because feminists tell us it is misogynistic, or because the LGBTQ+ crowd tells us its views on sexuality are evilly repressive, or because politicians tell us it has no place in the public square. We do not need to satisfy unbelieving minds, minds that hate God's revelation, whose reason is unmoored from reality. As Proverbs 21:30 tells us, "There is no wisdom or understanding or counsel against Yahweh."

If you are to understand who you are, why you are here, and what to do with it all, if you desire wisdom, *the* source for all wisdom is God himself who has revealed himself, his purposes, and his plans. The search for wisdom apart from God's revelation is futile, frustrating, fruitless, and ultimately ends in death.

Proverbs 4:20-27

My son, be attentive to my words;
  incline your ear to my sayings.
Let them not escape from your sight;
  keep them within your heart.
For they are life to those who find them,
  and healing to all their flesh.
Keep your heart with all vigilance,
  for from it flow the springs of life.
Put away from you crooked speech,
  and put devious talk far from you.
Let your eyes look directly forward,
  and your gaze be straight before you.
Ponder the path of your feet;
  then all your ways will be sure.
Do not swerve to the right or to the left;
  turn your foot away from evil.

CHAPTER 6

A Heart For Wisdom

Approaching the book of Proverbs as a superficial "how-to" manual for human relationships can be tempting. The book's practical wisdom saturates every page. People working in the field of behavioral psychology could benefit greatly from reading the book of Proverbs. Solomon gives us disciplines to employ that lead to productivity and long-term happiness. We are also given behaviors to avoid that are destructive. So, if we are not careful, we can read Proverbs like one might read *Atomic Habits* by James Clear, *12 Rules for Life* by Jordan Peterson, or *Extreme Ownership* by Jocko Willink and Leif Babin. These books (and other books like them) have much to commend them, but they are not Proverbs.

Proverbs is not merely a manual for superficial techniques. At the heart of the wisdom of Proverbs is the matter of the human heart. The wisdom that God requires of us runs deeper than a mere manipulation of our situations to turn things to our benefit. The wisdom that God calls for is a wisdom that captivates the heart.

The father wants his son to have a heart of wisdom and a heart for wisdom. The heart is not pitted against actions in Proverbs as if all God cares about is whether your heart is in the right place but he does not care about what you do. But for your works to be the manifestation of true wisdom, your heart must be tuned correctly. As Waltke comments, "A person could memorize the book of Proverbs and still lack wisdom if it did not affect his heart, which informs behavior."[1]

So, how do you learn wisdom? It all begins with the heart. The Scriptures in general and Proverbs in particular have much to say about the heart. What is the heart?

The Heart: Central Command

The heart is central command for your entire person. The Hebrew word translated "heart" often could be used synonymously with the "mind" (e.g., Prov 3:3; 6:32a; 7:7b). The mind is more than the brain. To have the mind of Christ, as Paul speaks about in 1 Corinthians 2 or Philippians 2, is not equivalent to having the brain of Christ. The mind involves the *way* we think as well as *what* we think, the way we see and respond to the world around us. We are

---

1. Waltke, Vol. 1, 77.

to be transformed by the renewing of our minds, Paul exhorts the Romans (Rom 12:1-2). Our brains are involved in our minds, but they are not the totality of our minds.

The heart involves the mind, but Proverbs also associates it with our emotions (Prov 15:15, 30), the will (11:20; 14:14) and the whole inner being (3:5). The heart, therefore, is the center of our being, mind, will, and emotions, that is the source of our affections and loyalties. The heart is the well-spring of your desires, and your desires determine your actions. What you desire most is your deepest allegiance, and your deepest allegiance will determine the way you think, speak, act, etc. The heart is the place where these deepest allegiances and desires reside, shaping everything about us.

If you want to know what or who has your heart, examine what you do, where your commitments are, what you avoid, and what you pursue. We always do what we desire most. Whatever we do reveals what we desire.

Let's think about this in terms of a common experience for many of us: I want to lose weight because I want all the pants in my closet to fit so I do not have to buy a new wardrobe. If this is my greatest desire in the area of my health, I will consistently avoid eating that pint of ice cream. Oh, I have a great desire for ice cream, but my greater desire is to lose weight, which controls all other desires. If I consistently eat the pint of ice cream, I know my greatest desire is to satisfy my present craving instead of focusing on my long-term goal. Ice cream has my heart.

This is not an illustration of choosing between sinful behavior (eating ice cream) and righteous behavior (not eating ice cream), but is intended simply as an analogy about how desires and heart loyalties work. What I want most is revealed by my actions.

Issues of the heart run much deeper and have greater consequences than the size of my waist. Solomon exhorts his son to guard his heart with all vigilance *for from it flows the springs of life* (Prov 4:23). All of life flows from the heart; from the seemingly inconsequential relationship with ice cream to your eternal destiny.

Your heart is command central to your entire person. Whatever or whoever has your heart has you. If you desire wisdom above folly, you will pursue wisdom above folly, even if occasionally you fall into folly. The heart is the place where wisdom and folly dictate life. The heart is the common factor between the wise and the fool. What each person does with his heart is what distinguishes them from another.

The difference between the wise man and the fool is not some intellectual capacity or ability. The fool does not lack mental equipment. He has a mind, will, and emotions. The fool may be extremely intellectually capable. But the fool, as we learn in Proverbs 1:7, despises wisdom and discipline. The fool is one whose mind, or heart, is closed to wisdom; he is stubborn, obstinate, refusing to listen. The fool's problem is an obedience problem, not a lack of mental capacity.

His heart is controlled by foolishness, a refusal to listen to God, to understand the difference between right and wrong, to put his world together apart from submission to God's blueprints. The fool rests in his own understanding without reference to God's wisdom.

One reason why Solomon gives instruction to his son in wisdom, and the reason we continue to need to be instructed in wisdom and instruct our children, is that we are all conceived and born as fools. Foolishness is bound up in our hearts from birth (Prov 22:15). This is not immaturity, but rebellion. We desire to do things our way, not submitting to God. Our hearts are overwhelmed, enslaved to foolishness from conception. This is why parents are called to discipline children, driving foolishness from their hearts with the rod and instructing them in the way of wisdom.

If the heart remains bound by foolishness, the destiny of the person will be destruction. All of life's direction and its final destiny are determined by the heart.

Because your temporal and eternal destinies are determined by the heart, because you cannot fulfill your purpose as the image of God without a wise heart, how do you develop a wise heart?

Cultivating a Heart for Wisdom

Your heart *can* be cultivated. It is not as though you are "stuck" with a foolish heart. Neither can you use God's sovereignty as an excuse for your heart's condition. We know from Proverbs and elsewhere in Scripture that God does determine heart conditions and direction. We hear it plainly in Proverbs 21:1: "The king's heart is a stream of water in the hand of Yahweh; he turns it wherever he will." Ultimately God's wise purpose is worked out sovereignly and unalterably. But Proverbs is equally as clear about our responsibility to cultivate our hearts.

How God works all this is a secret that belongs to him. The commands he has given us are our responsibilities (Deut 29:29). Your heart condition is your responsibility.

Think of it this way: Your whole person is a plot of ground, a garden whose soil has the potential of growing food and beautiful flowers or thorns and thistles. We know that God causes things to grow. But he works with those who are diligent in preparing the soil, planting, and watering. You will not have a good garden waiting on something to drop from heaven. If you are slothful about cultivating your heart, you will grow thorns and thistles.

It is no mere coincidence that Jesus uses horticultural imagery to speak about men and their hearts. For instance, in Luke 6, Jesus says:

> For no good tree bears bad fruit, nor again does a bad tree bear good fruit, for each tree is known by its own fruit. For figs are not gathered from thornbushes, nor are grapes picked from a bramble bush. The good person out of the good treasure of his heart produces good, and the evil person out of his evil treasure produces evil, for out of the abundance of the heart his mouth speaks. (Luke 6:43-35)

We are plots of ground, made from the dust of the earth, who are called to bear the proper type of fruit. God ordinarily works through the means he has ordained. In this case, he works on your heart when you employ the means he has provided for you to cultivate your heart. A person who uses God's sovereignty as an excuse for his laziness and disobedience blasphemes God. You are responsible for cultivating your heart. Your heart can change, being freed to a great degree from foolishness and become a heart of wisdom.

So, how is it done?

In Proverbs 4:20-27, the whole body with all its capacities is involved. You cultivate the heart by what you let in through your eyes and ears and where your feet take you.

> My son, be attentive to my words, incline your *ears* to my sayings. Let them not escape from your *sight,* keep them within your *heart.* For they are life to those who find them and healing to all their flesh… Let your *eyes* look directly forward, and your gaze be straight before you. Ponder the path of your *feet….*"

The whole person, the whole *body,* is involved in cultivating your heart. Wisdom comes from outside of you, through your ears and eyes, listening and seeing in places your feet have taken you. The wisdom you learn goes down into your heart where you make the decision of whether or not to treasure it. When you receive with the ear and through the eyes, you meditate on these things and they become a part of your heart.

The process also works the other way: What you have received through your feet taking you to places where you can hear and see wisdom, when wisdom gets inside of you, it comes out through your ears, eyes, and feet.

The Scriptures are *the* source for wisdom. So, your ears, eyes, and feet must be in a position to receive the

Scriptures—God's revelation of himself—the fear of the Lord. To cultivate a heart of wisdom, you must approach the Scriptures with humility, recognizing them as the wisdom of the all-wise God and willing to submit to them, which is nothing more than submission to God himself.

This process begins by *listening*, first to the Scriptures and also to those who communicate the Scriptures and their applications to you. Solomon calls on his son to be attentive and incline his ear to instruction. Listening to the Scriptures involves reading them or listening to them read and taught. Listening does not simply entail placing yourself in a position so that sound waves hit your ear. Listening is a discipline that seeks understanding of what is said, not imposing on the speaker only what I want him to say. When you approach the Scriptures, you must hear them for what they actually say and not what you or anyone else wants them to say.

Because of the foolishness in our hearts, we have a proclivity to seek the justification of our actions by twisting Scriptures. Today this is especially a temptation in the church as it concerns homosexuality. People have "vile affections," as Paul calls them in Romans 1, but they seek to justify them by twisting the Scriptures to express approval of homosexuality. Unfortunately, many professing Christians have joined the broader culture to declare a new gospel: "Love is love no matter who you love." The Bible can be interpreted, or discarded, according to this new gospel. Any and all such relationships, governed by this new love, are legitimate. You can build a family and society that flourishes by endorsing and even praising such relationships governed by this new love. In fact, you can celebrate these deviancies with an entire month called "Pride Month" and only expect that good things will be the consequence. But that is not *listening* to Scripture.

Whether you hear the Scriptures directly or you hear teachers (parents, pastors, friends) communicating the truth and wisdom of Scripture, you must be a good listener. If what you are hearing is not directly from Scripture, discernment is required, but if Scripture supports what you hear, you must heed it as your father's instruction.

Another requirement for cultivating a heart of wisdom is *allegiance to God or faith in God.* Proverbs 3:5-6 says, "Trust in Yahweh with all your heart, and do not lean on your own understanding. In all your ways acknowledge him, and he will make straight your paths." To cultivate a heart of wisdom, there must be a fundamental allegiance to God. This allegiance is the "fear of the Lord," and this is the beginning of wisdom (9:10). This allegiance listens to God in humility, refusing to exalt your knowledge against the knowledge of God.

I have heard some interpret "lean not on your own understanding" as some type of indictment against being educated or intelligent. It is nothing of the sort. God is not calling you to some blind, unintelligent faith.

What does it mean to lean not on your own understanding? You do not lean completely on your own understanding because you know your knowledge is limited and, therefore, incomplete. What looks like a really good decision or course of action may be a way of destruction because you do not have all the necessary knowledge. Perspective and fuller knowledge are needed to make good decisions. When God says, "Trust me, you don't want to do that," you should trust him.

Let's think about this in terms of driving. A map shows you the shortest route to your destination is by taking a certain road. The person with whom you are riding has been traveling this route for years and tells you, "Yeah, that road is the shortest distance, but the bridge is out. You can't get there by taking that road. Take this other road." Who are you going to trust? Hopefully the guy with greater knowledge.

Besides our limited knowledge, we also have the handicap of sin that distorts our thinking. These two factors together can be devastating.

For example, you may notice a young lady is gorgeous, and she is showing interest in you. Your dad and mom, however, see some concerning character issues, informed by their understanding of Scriptures and their experience. Do you trust what God has revealed about the character of Harlot Folly and how your parents are guiding you with that wisdom, or do you lean on your own understanding, thinking you can make a housewife out of a harlot?

Or another example: That young man is exciting, a bad boy. He goes to church, but he has character issues; he is irresponsible, a sloth. He has shown interest in you, and you are the envy of all the other girls. In that moment you come up with all sorts of reasoning as to why it would be good for you and him to be together. You can change him. Are you going to listen to wisdom about the character of a sloth, or will you lean on your own understanding?

God has perspective that you do not have and will never have. It is not that he does not want you to be smart.

Quite the opposite. It is stupidest, most ignorant thing you can do in failing to trust the one who knows everything, who sees the end of all decisions.

As Solomon tells us throughout Proverbs, we are going to be tempted from every direction, called by Harlot Folly, or the gang of blood thirsty, greedy boys, or by our own proclivities toward evil. Our limitations as well as our sins will encourage us to make decisions that are, at best, short-sighted and, at worst, completely destructive. This is why your fundamental commitment, your heart, must belong to Yahweh, committing your way to him so that he can direct your paths. Your heart's allegiance to Yahweh will help subdue your urges, keeping them in control, and keeping everything in proper perspective.

Another activity of cultivating a heart for wisdom that cannot be overlooked is that this cultivation will take *work*. Hear what the father says to his son on several occasions:

"The heart of him who has understanding *seeks* knowledge" (Prov 15:14).

"An intelligent heart acquires knowledge, and the ear of the wise *seeks* knowledge" (18:15).

"Incline your ear, and hear the words of the wise, and *apply* your heart to my knowledge" (22:17).

"*Apply* your heart to instruction and your ear to words of knowledge" (23:12).

> "Hear, my son, and be wise, and *direct* your heart in the way" (23:19).

> "My son, if you receive my words and *treasure up* my commandments with you, *making your ear attentive* to wisdom and *inclining your heart* to understanding; yes, if you call out for insight and raise your voice for understanding, if you *seek* it like silver and *search* for it as for hidden treasures, then you will understand the fear of Yahweh and find the knowledge of God" (2:1-5).

Do you hear all of those action verbs? They all speak of work: Treasure up, make your ear attentive, incline your heart, seek, apply, direct, search. You have to go out and find wisdom. This requires focus, effort, determination, perseverance. Wisdom is learned in pursuit.

Lest we think this pursuit of God is defined purely in the old pietistic way—namely, that it is all about some spiritual breakthrough—pursuing Wisdom, God himself, means joining him in his work through prayer and listening to his word. But pursuing wisdom also involves taking on responsibilities in the world that aid in the man's mission in the world. The effort is about taking risks as well as spending time in prayer; it is about pursuing new adventures as well as learning the Scriptures.

You want to learn wisdom? Pursue marriage; take the risk. You want to learn wisdom? Start that business, take that promotion, tackle that project, have those children, or learn that new skill. See areas of creation that are disordered and seek to bring order to them.

Are you a man or a woman? There are particular callings for each and some things you cannot do and some things you should not do. Where are you in the world? Illinois, Texas, Russia, China, or India? What are your resources: finances, time, abilities? Take all those factors into consideration, but *act*. Try something. Take the risk. There will be failures, disappointments, and frustrations along the way, but that is how you cultivate wisdom and become a better ruler of God's creation.

All this circles back to a common assumption in Proverbs: *personal responsibility*. Solomon calls on his son to hear and do these things. But he can only instruct and guide. Solomon presents the two ways of wisdom and folly. His son must choose what he will do with what he hears.

This is a good reminder in an age in which we blame everything else and everyone else but ourselves for how our lives turn out. Sure, bad things happened. But what are you going to do about it right now? You made bad choices. Other people made bad choices that affected you. There are many things that are outside of our control. Granted. What are you doing with the things over which you have control? Are you wallowing in self-pity and depression because you do not like the consequences of your choices or the consequences of what others have done, or are you owning what you can and doing what you can to make things better?

Sitting there and wishing life had been better or being consumed with regret is a waste of time and energy. You have to take responsibility for what you can do and start sorting out things the best you can at this time, being committed to the long haul, making wise decisions, which means not always deciding on something that will give you immediate relief from pain and suffering but will pay bigger and better dividends in the end. No shortcuts. No immediate gratification without thinking of the long-term effects. No staying in the same place because this happens to be where you feel most comfortable even though it would be wiser to pursue a different path. In order to cultivate wisdom, you must first take the responsibility to be a student of wisdom, pursuing wisdom wherever she may be found.

Developing a heart of wisdom also means *owning* wisdom. In other words, these are not superficial techniques learned in a seminar on how to run your business better. This is not mere pragmatism. As we hear in Proverbs 2:1 and 4:21, wisdom's words and ways must be treasured and guarded in your heart. The knowledge you receive must be your reality. This is the way you see and interact with the world around you.

Where God says, "This is wrong," you put that in your heart. Where God says, "This is right," you put that in your heart. You must speak, work, and walk according to what you have learned. God's word, will, and ways must own your deepest allegiance, shaping your desires and directing your thoughts, will, emotions, and actions.

All of this is related to *applying* or *walking* in wisdom's way. Your hands must work to shape things according to wisdom. Your feet must walk wisdom's path. The more you apply wisdom, the more you grow in wisdom. The more you grow in wisdom, the more your heart is given to wisdom.

Think of what happens when you tentatively and maybe reluctantly start some diet and exercise program or even endeavor in a new business venture. You begin by disciplining yourself to do the right things. As you progress and begin seeing the results of this discipline, you begin to enjoy these things more, becoming more convinced of the benefits, and they begin to shape your desires even more. When you begin to see the benefits of wisdom's way, you develop a more receptive heart for wisdom.

An amazing transformation happens over time as you cultivate a heart for wisdom. Though you will always be tempted with folly and sin, it becomes less and less appealing.

Somewhere along the way, you look at people who have chosen the way of folly and wonder, "What are you thinking? That's insane." You are not arrogant about it, but you really do not understand why someone would want to live a self-destructive life. Your heart is given to wisdom's way. It is a process. It will take time and persevering effort.

Wisdom is not an abstract principle, a set of propositions to guide the minds of men. Wisdom, as we learned early on is a person. Jesus Christ is wisdom from God (1 Cor 1:30).

Christ, Our Wisdom

Everything revealed as wisdom in the book of Proverbs is the revelation of Christ Jesus, who is wisdom. Cultivating a heart for wisdom is cultivating a heart for Christ. To know wisdom you must know Christ Jesus. In Christ Jesus, God has revealed reality. In him all things hold together (Col

1:17). In him we see the fullness of who God is, the way you relate to him, and the way the world works. In Christ are hidden all of the treasures of wisdom and knowledge (Col 2:3)

Christ Jesus, who is Wisdom, must control your affections, loyalties, and actions. Christ must have your deepest allegiances. He must have your heart. You must trust in Jesus with all your heart and lean not on your own understanding, in all your ways acknowledge him, and he will direct your paths. You must, as Paul says in Romans 10, confess with your mouth that Jesus is Lord and believe in your heart that God raised him from the dead to be saved.

The challenge is, as Paul makes clear in 1 Corinthians 1, that God's revelation of wisdom through a crucified Christ is foolishness to the world. The world outside of Christ believes reality can be ordered in a different way, that relationships between men and with the non-human creation can be arranged according to a human understanding that rejects the revelation of God in Christ.

You must listen to Jesus humbly, receiving his words. Your deepest loyalty must be to him and his ways. You must cultivate your relationship with him through persevering effort.

The world believes it is foolishness to deny yourself any pleasure that is within your reach. To them it is foolishness to trust in the unseen promise of pleasure in the future. Self-denial and trusting the word of the Scriptures seems foolish to them.

These are the proverbs of the world:

"God wants you to be happy. You should do whatever makes you happy right now. If that means mutilating your body because you don't like your sex, divorcing your spouse because he/she doesn't make you happy, sleeping around, pursuing a career instead of motherhood, being a player instead of a responsible husband and father, getting into mounds of debt, you should do it and know that God approves because he wants you to be happy."

"You say whatever you feel. That is your right."

"Discomfort is the greatest evil. Do whatever you must to avoid any and all discomfort."

"You are perfect just the way you are. Don't let anyone tell you differently."

"You are not evil. Guns are evil, drugs are evil, your parents are evil, society is evil, and they are all to blame for your condition."

Consider the world's proverbs in light of what God has revealed to us: "There is a way that seems right unto a man, but its end is the way of death" (Prov 14:12; 16:25) The world's wisdom leads to death, but God's wisdom—Jesus—is resurrection life.

If you follow the wisdom of God, you will be counted a fool by the world. Stay the course. Do not waver. Continue to cultivate a heart for Christ, the wisdom of God.

Proverbs 4

Hear, O sons, a father's instruction,
and be attentive, that you may gain insight,
for I give you good precepts;
do not forsake my teaching.
When I was a son with my father,
tender, the only one in the sight of my mother,
he taught me and said to me,
"Let your heart hold fast my words;
keep my commandments, and live.
Get wisdom; get insight;
do not forget, and do not turn away from the words of my
mouth.
Do not forsake her, and she will keep you;
love her, and she will guard you.
The beginning of wisdom is this: Get wisdom,
and whatever you get, get insight.
Prize her highly, and she will exalt you;
she will honor you if you embrace her.
She will place on your head a graceful garland;
she will bestow on you a beautiful crown."
Hear, my son, and accept my words,
that the years of your life may be many.
I have taught you the way of wisdom;
I have led you in the paths of uprightness.
When you walk, your step will not be hampered,

and if you run, you will not stumble.
Keep hold of instruction; do not let go;
  guard her, for she is your life.
Do not enter the path of the wicked,
  and do not walk in the way of the evil.
Avoid it; do not go on it;
  turn away from it and pass on.
For they cannot sleep unless they have done wrong;
  they are robbed of sleep unless they have made someone
  stumble.
For they eat the bread of wickedness
  and drink the wine of violence.
But the path of the righteous is like the light of dawn,
  which shines brighter and brighter until full day.
The way of the wicked is like deep darkness;
  they do not know over what they stumble.

CHAPTER 7

Wisdom for Parents

In Western society, youth is idolized. There is a constant quest to hold on to youth throughout our lives—everything from keeping up with the latest cultural trends and tech to surgically altering our bodies. We want to stay forever young. The great sin is getting old and being like your parents. This was depicted in a series of television commercials for Progressive Insurance. The theme of the commercials was, "Don't become like your parents." In one commercial, an older man is teaching young adults how not to become like their parents when they become homeowners. There are some things to laugh about in the commercials because we all, at every age, have our quirks that are funny. But there is also something that is sinister about it. Why would you not want to be like your parents? Why would you not want to look at the patterns of their lives and listen to them speak to you from experience, especially when that experience has a righteous perspective?

The Bible is not opposed to age, or ageist. The one who is all-wise is the Ancient of Days, the old one. It is precisely his maturity that makes him the best one to arrange the world as it ought to be as well as the source of wisdom, deserving a hearing from all. We must act like our older brother and grow up to be like our father. It should come as no surprise, then, that God calls for the young people listening to learn from those who are older than them, particularly, but not exclusively, from their parents. Parents are God's primary mouthpiece for wisdom in his created order, teaching children from their infancy. This is a burden, a responsibility, for both parents and children as we shall see.

Parents: Conveyers of Wisdom

Though the fundamental and ultimate source of wisdom is divine revelation, God has ordained other means through which we are taught wisdom. Proverbs indicates other ways in which we learn wisdom. The principal communicators of wisdom in Proverbs are the father and mother. There are many proverbs about fatherly, or parental, instruction throughout the book, but this is not a theme you have to piece together from scattered verses. Proverbs *is* fatherly instruction. Proverbs is a father instructing his son in wisdom and discipline (Prov 1:2-6). Addresses to "my son" or "sons" are found throughout the book. Proverbs is a catechism for youth, especially young men, taught by fathers and mothers.

Proverbs assumes a child's father, or parents, will be present in their lives, which may not be the case for many in today's world. I will speak later about how the fatherless can obtain fatherly wisdom, but there is nothing that can replace your father. America is learning this the hard way.

According to one study, approximately thirty-five percent of children under eighteen live in a single-parent home as of 2016. As many as twenty-five percent of children in the country live in households with a mother alone. That is more than eighteen million children who do not live with a father.[1] Fatherlessness is an epidemic. Sixty-three percent of youth suicides, ninety percent of all homeless and runaway youths, seventy-one percent of all high school dropouts, seventy percent of juveniles in state-operated institutions, and seventy-five percent of adolescent patients in substance abuse centers have fatherlessness in common.[2]

The problem is especially acute in the black communities, which, oddly enough, was not nearly as much of a problem before the Civil Rights Movement and the War on Poverty. Larry Elder, a black conservative talk show host and attorney, surmised that the three biggest problems facing the black community are 1) lack of fathers in the home, 2) lack of fathers in the home, and 3) lack of fathers in the home.[3] Mothers are predominantly the single-parent with

---

1. Wayne Parker, "Statistics on Fatherless Children in America," Liveabout, accessed June 22, 2021, https://www.liveabout.com/fatherless-children-in-america-statistics-1270392?print.

2. Ibid.

3. Larry Elder (@larryelder), "The Top Three Biggest Problems Facing The Black Community 1) Lack of fathers in the home

only eight percent of single parent homes being father-only.[4]

There are many factors contributing to this disheartening trend: Feminism, the sexual revolution, welfare replacing fathers, divorce courts predominantly deferring to mothers, and many other factors. Whatever the causes, these are the cultural waters in which we are swimming, the atmosphere we are breathing, and all this affects our lives even if we do not see it as prominently in our local church. In God's providence, this is the society in which God has called Westerners to live in the twenty-first century, calling us to set before this society the way of wisdom by the way we order our homes.

Fathers and husbands, the greatest burden for this responsibility for teaching and leading the home in wisdom belongs to you. This begins by taking up your responsibilities to keep your family together by being what God called you to be and setting the course for your family. Your presence is vital. It is not the wife or mother's home in which you are a "second adult," or a guest, or—worse—another one of the children for whom she has to care. Your wife and children need you to be a father: strong, calm, leading, directing, and providing. In the division of labor, your wife may do a great deal more *in* the home, but she cannot do

2) Lack of fathers in the home 3) Lack of fathers in the home But let's talk about the allegedly "racist" @realDonaldtrump...," Twitter, August 17, 2018, 7:40 p.m., https://twitter.com/larry-elder/status/1030615507391660032.

4. Parker, "Statistics on Fatherless Children"

what you do *for* the home. She cannot replace you, nor can you replace her. We are not exchangeable.

Wives and mothers, you also must answer the calling God has given you to work in line with the godly mission of your husband and create peace in the home. It takes both of you to create a good culture in the home. It only takes one of you to tear it to pieces.

The need for both fathers and mothers in rearing a wise child is evident throughout Proverbs.

Parental Complementarianism

We hear in several places that it is both the instruction of father and mother that play a part in wise child rearing. Speaking of the father and mother's instruction is how Solomon begins the heart of the book: "Hear, my son, your father's instruction, and forsake not your mother's teaching" (Prov 1:8). And he echoes this point again in Proverbs 6:20: "My son, keep your father's commandment, and forsake not your mother's teaching." Once more in Proverbs 23:22: "Listen to your father who gave you life, and do not despise your mother when she is old." Conclusion: A child has the best chance to grow in wisdom when he has instruction from father and mother—masculine and feminine instruction.

Fathers and mothers bring different, but complementary views on the world, each with valuable perspectives, both of which are good for sons and daughters in learning how to relate to the world around them. Men and women approach the world differently based on the way God created them, and those differences complement one another so that the overall mission given to them can be completed.

Men approach the world prioritizing rationality over emotion, oriented toward the dirt from which they were created, taking risks, engaging the world, trying to solve problems with *things*. Man is not an emotionless creature. God has wired his brain and his person, however, to prioritize rationality over emotion in order to get things done.

Women prioritize emotion over rationality. This does not mean they are irrational, though some men think so when they compare them to themselves. Women are created from the man and oriented to the man. They prioritize emotional connections and relationships, always wanting to make sure everyone is nurtured and cared for, that there is peace.

All this is expressed in parenting. Dads parent "more dangerously," as I have heard it said. They play rougher and encourage risk-taking. They are the ones throwing the children in the pool or lake saying, "Sink or swim," teaching the children to learn how to overcome their fears. Dads tend to be more stern in discipline, expecting performance, stressing rules, justice, fairness, and duty, giving children a keen sense of right and wrong. Dads help prepare children for challenges, toughening them up mentally, emotionally, and physically so they do not get crushed in a merciless world. Dads encourage competition and engender independence.

Moms want to provide safety and a sense of security, providing sympathy, care, and help, emphasizing the importance of relationships. As one author says, "Dads tend to see their child in relation to the rest of the world. Moms tend to see the rest of the world in relation to their child."[5] The emotional bond created between mother and child at birth through age three is vital to the emotional well-being of the child in the long run.

Neither mother nor father is superior or inferior to the other as though we were comparing two of the same thing. Both mother and father are needed perspectives. Think about it in terms of a son injuring himself and the different responses of the parents. Though boy moms may become conditioned to injuries over time, the reactions from the dad and mom are generally distinct.

Dad: "I've had worse in my eyeball. No bones are sticking out. Shake it off and stop your crying."

Mom: "Let me look at that. Oh, I know it hurts. I will take care of it, but you do need to calm down. Let me give you a hug."

If there is only dad's perspective, the boy can become a heartless, hardened sociopath. If there is only mom's perspective, he can become effeminate. Dads are tough and moms are nurturing. Our sons and daughters need both. Male and female perspectives are both needed for wisdom because God has created male and female in relationship with one another as the means to complete man's mission in the world. To rear a wise child, there is a need for both.

---

5. "The Significance of a Father's Influence," Focus on the Family, 2011, https://www.focusonthefamily.com/family-qa/ the-significance-of-a-fathers-influence/.

Parental Responsibility and Authority

Actively training your children in the ways of discipline is not an option. Parental responsibility is assumed throughout Proverbs, but there also are direct commands given to the mother and father.

Several times we hear the direct command, "Discipline your son" (Prov 19:18; 29:17; also 23:13). The command to discipline the son assumes you have both the responsibility and authority to do so. God never gives responsibility where he does not also give authority. As parents you have the authority to command and correct your children.

This is not absolute authority so that whatever you do is right. As parents, you are accountable to other authorities so that you do not abuse your authority. Nevertheless, the authority you have is real and must be used for the purpose of shaping and guiding your children so they grow in wisdom.

Where God has given you authority, he has given you responsibility. You are to use your authority to teach your children the way of wisdom. Every child is a special calling from God.

God called us to fruitfulness, and fruitfulness involves as much *quality* as it does *quantity*. Have a great number of children. The Scriptures encourage it. But that is not where the encouragement stops. Sometimes we treat children like puppies: We like them when they are infants and cute, but we lose interest when they become much more difficult to deal with as they get older. God has not called you *either* to have many children *or* to rear wise children. He has called you to both. If you have a dozen children and baptize them all but neglect to discipline so they turn out to be thorns and thistles, you haven't been fruitful. Thorns are not life-giving fruit. They only exacerbate the problem of death. If you have children, you must take responsibility to train them. You cannot turn them out like free-range chickens.

Every time you have another child, you may need to cut off certain activities you like to do in order to fulfill your responsibilities. If that is the case, that is what you must do. We are limited creatures that cannot do it all or have it all. You must make choices, and when it comes to child-rearing, the choice has been made for you: Train your child in wisdom.

God has given you all the tools you need to provide this discipline and instruction for your children.

Parental Tools: The condition of the child

As parents, we are given *knowledge of the condition of our children.* Proverbs 22:15 says, "Folly is bound up in the heart of a child." Your child is not an exception to this truth. I was always amazed when people spoke of our young children as though we "got some good ones," as though our children came from the womb praying the Lord's Prayer, fully self-disciplined. We were diligent in the discipline of our children because we recognized foolishness was bound up in their hearts.

Like their parents, they were and remain sinners.

Wise children make parents' hearts glad and provide rest (Prov 27:11; 29:17), but when left untended, those little plots of earth will become thorns and thistles that will be the bane of your existence, causing you grief beyond what you can imagine.

On several occasions in Proverbs we are told something to the effect of what we find in Proverbs 17:25, "A foolish son is a grief to his father and bitterness to her who bore him" (see also Prov 10:1; 15:20).

Foolishness in Proverbs is not ignorant immaturity but rebellion against God. Even Jesus had to learn and mature, growing in wisdom (Luke 2:52). There are things we do not know that we need to learn. We need parents with perspective and experience grounded in the Scriptures to give guidance in overcoming ignorance.

Foolishness is not innocent immaturity. Foolishness is rebellion, a natural inclination to disobey God and all those who represent him. This is the inheritance of our first father, passed to every generation. Our hearts are corrupt and must be corrected. The people who must first recognize this in the relationship are the parents, not assuming their children are coming out of the womb uncorrupted. God has provided you wisdom concerning the nature of your child. Work with it.

Teaching tools

God has even authorized the use of certain tools to help drive out this foolishness from their hearts. To complete the verse I began earlier, "Folly is bound up in the heart of a child, but the rod of discipline drives it far from him" (Prov 22:15). The rod is an instrument that brings physical pain. I know that in an age in which discomfort is one of the greatest sins (or an age when abuse is common), some do not like the idea of inflicting physical pain.

Though there are various forms of discipline that can be employed with the principle of pain as a consequence for stepping out of line, I do not think we ought to discount or dismiss physical pain. Proverbs 20:30 says, "Blows that wound cleanse away evil; strokes make clean the innermost parts." There is a connection between physical pain and the mind and heart. Psychological pain is bad and can be effective. But the Scriptures connect the body's pain with the heart.

There are physical, painful consequences when one does not walk in the way of wisdom. When consequences come from a loving hand in a measured way that also is intended to correct and not destroy, the consequence is transformed into a help. If the consequences are not imposed by a loving hand in a measured way, they will later come from an unloving hand in an unmeasured way as a grown-up fool is beaten in many ways.

If you love your children, you *will* correct them with some form of painful discipline. Proverbs is quite clear that, "Whoever spares the rod hates his son, but he who loves him is diligent to discipline him" (Prov 13:24). Like God himself, you show your delight in your beloved son when you discipline him (Prov 3:11-12). The rod is a God-given parental tool to deliver your child from the death of a fool (Prov 23:14; 19:18). If you love your child, you will endure the short-term pain for the long-term gain.

The rod, however, is not your only tool. It must be coupled with reproof and instruction in righteousness. If a child has no instruction through words and example, the rod will be seen as an arbitrary tool for the parent to vent his frustration. There needs to be positive as well as corrective discipline, instruction as well as punishment.

None of this works like magic. There are no certain outcomes, there is only faithfulness in fulfilling parental responsibility and the response of the child.

The sufficiency of parental discipline

God has given you, as parents, the responsibility to reveal and lead your children to the path of wisdom. Parental wisdom, though not exhaustive, is sufficient to rear wise children. God has given every child imperfect parents who are learning along the way.

We can and should learn from those who are older than us, whether through some type of mentorship or by reading what our ancestors have left us, but no one reared *these* children. Every child is unique in some ways and requires particular training.

There are many times we, as parents, feel the weight of responsibility and the consequent sense of inadequacy as parents. God gave these children to *you*. He has told you that you are their principal source of teaching and made promises to you about teaching your children. Your parenting is not going to be perfect. You yourself are still growing in knowledge as well as dealing with sin in your own life.

But God would not have made you parents if you were not adequate for the task. Your only challenge is to seek to be as faithful as you possibly can with the knowledge that you have in rearing your children. Your responsibility is to do the best you know to do at the time of child-rearing.

A word to parents who look back with regrets: Hindsight being what it is, it is easy to look back with greater perspective and experience and judge your former selves to see where you were deficient. Your child or children strayed when they got older, so you review your history of parenting. You see the mistakes that were made. But here are the questions you need to be asking yourselves: Did I do what I believed was best at the time with the knowledge I had, seeking to be faithful to God? When you are in the situation, you simply do not know what you do not know. You only know what you know at the time. God is going to hold you accountable for what you did with what he gave you at the time. If you were diligent, trying to learn, receiving counsel, and seeking to apply it as faithfully as possible, that is what God requires of you. Were you faithful with the knowledge you had at the time? The second question is, "Were you unfaithful with the knowledge you had at the time?" If you neglected your children's training because you were pursuing other things, if you were lazy and did not apply what you knew, you need to ask for forgiveness from your children.

Parental training is sufficient for children to learn the way of wisdom. But there is also an insufficiency of parental discipline.

Insufficiency of parental discipline

Parental discipline is not enough to make a wise child. No parenting is foolproof—literally. The best parent ever, God the Father, had a wayward son (Adam) even after he gave him a perfect environment, tools, and instruction. Children have responsibility to respond to the instruction. You cannot make them.

There is a recognition in Proverbs that even the wisest child-rearing does not ensure wisdom.

> Wisdom can only encourage the child to seek it (e.g., Prov 2:1ff.).
>
> "A wise son hears his father's instruction, but a scoffer does not listen to rebuke" (13:1).
>
> Good homes sometimes produce sloths (10:5) or profligate sons (29:3).
>
> A child may rebel (15:20), mock (30:17), or curse (30:11; 20:20) his parents.
>
> Some parents form shameful children to be sure (29:15), but the child himself must bear his own blame (29:3; 2:2ff.).[6]

Children young and old, hear me: Your parents are not perfect; your situation is not always what you want it to be, but you are still responsible for your actions. I recognize as much as anyone how upbringing has long-term effects on us. I get it. However, for some reason, in God's providence, he gave you this battle to fight, whether it was the loss of a parent through death or divorce or just misguided or igno-

---

6. Derek Kidner, *Tyndale Old Testament Commentaries: Proverbs*, Vol. 17 (Downers Grove, IL: InterVarsity Press, 2008), 47.

rant parents who did their best but just did not know any better.

You still have a choice to make: Are you going to sit there and whine the rest of your life about all the ways your parents failed you, using it as an excuse to be slothful and not pursue the way of wisdom, or are you going to join the battle and walk the difficult path of wisdom? Some older children especially do not want to take responsibility for their own sins, laying the guilt on their parents, when they are fully capable of making the right choices now. Even the best of parents can only show you the way. You must choose to walk it.

Parents have their responsibility and children have theirs. Neither is to be neglected.

At this point, there might be some disagreement about the sufficiency of parenting. Despite all the proverbs about the possibility of wise parents raising a scoffer, Proverbs 22:6 says, "Train up a child in the way he should go; even when he is old he will not depart from it." That sounds like a guarantee. If I am faithful in rearing my child, even if he strays for a while, he will come back. If he never comes back, that means my sin is the cause for it. Another reading interprets the verse as a general principle that does not hold true in every case. Proverbs 22:6 is not a promise but a general principle.

Other ways of reading this verse fit more into the context of Proverbs. What is commonly translated "in the way he should go" is more literally, "according to his way." This could mean "according to his nature," which may include everything from whether or not the child is male or female to working with his individual personality. The phrasing is strange if Solomon is emphasizing training the child in the way of wisdom. "According to his way" is not the way Solomon normally speaks about training in the way of wisdom.

In my estimation, it is better to understand this proverb as speaking about knowing your child and "working with the grain" so that he is set for life to accomplish his mission. Parents train the child according to his personality, gifts, potential as well as his maturity level. He builds upon those fundamentals for the rest of his life. This discipline includes walking in the way of wisdom, but I do not believe Solomon is promising too much—the persevering faithfulness of every child. The context of the whole book speaks against it.

So, what if you had bad parents or no parents, or parents who did not train you at all? Are you completely without any kind of parental wisdom? No.

Not the gang

One temptation for the son is turning to the wrong source or mouthpiece for wisdom. Wisdom is not in the gang. In Proverbs 1, Solomon—speaking with his wife—instructs his son to avoid the enticement of "sinners," who, in this case, is a gang of peers (Prov 1:10ff.). The gang is enticing because they are exciting, doing cool things, demonstrating power. This is especially appealing for young men.

Note, though, that the gang always has a hierarchy because hierarchies naturally develop in relationships. This is not a God-ordained hierarchy established for the teaching of wisdom. The gang becomes a rival to father and mother, a contrast that Solomon makes clear when he tells his son to listen to his father and mother and *not* the gang.

Peers may be good friends. We all need them. When we are young—and Solomon is addressing a *young* man— even our good peers do not have the wisdom of the aged. This does not mean youthful peers cannot be helpful or even wise in some respects, but they are in the same stage of maturity. Youthful wisdom should be vetted by aged wisdom. Wisdom comes with age and experience grounded in divine revelation. Those who walk with the wise will be wise, but the companion of fools will be destroyed (Prov 13:20).

It is good for children to have friends of the same age, but when making decisions about what to do, they need to seek instruction from their parents. Friends who are your children's age do not know what they think they know. That is not an insult. It is reality. And they need to be humble enough to recognize reality and trust their parents' wisdom.

Family Near and Far

What if your parents are not available to you, for whatever reason? What do you do? You do not turn to the gang, but you can turn to others.

Sometimes, thankfully, there are grandparents to whom young children can turn. If you have grandparents as well as parents, especially if they are faithful, it is good just to sit and visit with them at times, listening to their stories and hearing what they have to say about life. Do not despise their age. You will be wiser for it.

As Christians, our family also extends to others. Jesus went so far as to say his mother and brothers were those who did the will of his father (Matt 12:46-50). Paul referred to Timothy and Titus as his children (1 Tim 1:2; 2 Tim 1:2; Titus 1:4). We have parents in the faith, alive and dead. We can learn from mentors, traditions, and written works. We have the church, our mother, who guides us through pastors, elders, and various types of teachers.

Perhaps someone might respond, "No one can replace the biological father and mother! It is best if they are the ones who rear the child!" Of course, in a world unaffected by sin, this is the ideal. But we do not live in an ideal world. All sorts of things happen that make wise parental instruction difficult.

A person's particular situation may not be ideal with a biological father and mother who are faithful and live to a ripe old age, seeing their children's children, but God has provided parental wisdom from fathers and mothers in the faith. Those sources of wisdom may be more hidden from you than they are from other people, but God hides things, not because he does not like you, but because he is giving you a challenge to search out things (Prov 25:2). Be diligent.

God has made the supply of wisdom abundant through his revelation and our relationships to parents and church. There are consequences in both receiving and following wisdom as well as rejecting and not following wisdom.

Accepting Parental Wisdom

I can only comment on these briefly, but accepting parental wisdom makes glad parents.

> Listen to your father who gave you life, and do not despise your mother when she is old. Buy truth, and do not sell it; buy wisdom, instruction, and understanding. The father of the righteous will greatly rejoice; he who fathers a wise son will be glad in him. Let your father and mother be glad; let her who bore you rejoice (Prov 23:22-25)

Why is it a motivation for the son to seek the gladness of his father and mother? We are created with the need for approval. When God created the world, at various points during the creation week he declared each work good. Our relationship with God and our desire to hear him declare that we are good, accepted, in the right, beautiful in his eyes, beloved, etc., is what we long for. It is a natural need. God's principal representatives in our lives are our father and mother. They are the first ones to reveal God to us. We all long for our parents to tell us, "Well done!" Faithful parents are made glad and respond this way when you choose the way of wisdom. If you do not, they cannot show approval, and that leaves a gaping hole in your life you will seek to have filled in other ways.

Rejecting Parental Wisdom

Proverbs 30:11-14, 17 outlines what happens when there is a generation that curses their fathers and does not bless their mothers; they are arrogant, and their teeth become as swords devouring the poor from off of the earth. The eye that mocks a father and scorns to obey a mother will be picked out by the ravens of the valley and eaten by the vultures. Rejecting parental wisdom, especially when it is widespread, creates a violent society. They are subject to the curse of the covenant, becoming food for the birds (Deut 28:26).

In particular, the eyes of the rebellious are plucked out. That may happen physically, but the proverb seems to indicate that dishonoring your parents will impair your ability to judge. When given light, your eyes distinguish or judge between which way to walk, what to do, and what to avoid. They are instruments of judgment both physically and metaphorically. Rejecting parental wisdom will cause you to walk in the darkness of blindness, not being able to make good decisions, losing touch with reality, not being able to tell boys from girls, not understanding the necessity of work over handouts to fulfill our purpose—in short, you cannot see that all your wisdom is foolishness.

So, children, obey your parents in the Lord for this is right. Fathers, do not provoke your children to wrath but bring them up in the culture and instruction of the Lord.

Proverbs 1:8-19

Hear, my son, your father's instruction,
  and forsake not your mother's teaching,
for they are a graceful garland for your head
  and pendants for your neck.
My son, if sinners entice you,
  do not consent.
If they say, "Come with us, let us lie in wait for blood;
  let us ambush the innocent without reason;
like Sheol let us swallow them alive,
  and whole, like those who go down to the pit;
we shall find all precious goods,
  we shall fill our houses with plunder;
throw in your lot among us;
  we will all have one purse"—
my son, do not walk in the way with them;
  hold back your foot from their paths,
for their feet run to evil,
  and they make haste to shed blood.
For in vain is a net spread
  in the sight of any bird,
but these men lie in wait for their own blood;
  they set an ambush for their own lives.
Such are the ways of everyone who is greedy for unjust gain;
  it takes away the life of its possessors.

Proverbs 13:20

Whoever walks with the wise becomes wise,
but the companion of fools will suffer harm.

CHAPTER 8

Friendly Wisdom

Once upon a time there were two ladies and a young man. As young men do, he noticed both ladies. But one of these ladies was more noticeable than the other. Her attractiveness was captivating immediately. She accentuated herself in such a way as to catch the eye of the young man. She was a walking party, a good time waiting to happen. She dressed provocatively and was brazenly flirtatious. She invited him—and other young men as well—to throw off all restraint, forget about long-term consequences, and just live in the moment. Immediate pleasure was her promise. The young man was drawn to this woman.

But there was another woman. She was not so flashy, but she was attractive; indeed, she was beautiful. She was not loud and obnoxious like the first lady, nor did she dress to catch the lustful eye of men. She was modest in dress and speech. Her demeanor and her words were inviting, but to get to know her would take time and effort. Meeting her did not guarantee immediate pleasure. Pleasure would be had if the young man embraced her, but it would be the deep and fulfilling pleasure that only comes from reaching a destination after a long journey. Her beauty may not have been as eye-catching as the other lady, but if the young man would take the time, her beauty would be deeper and richer than the superficial attractiveness of the first lady.

Which woman will he choose? You tell me. The story is all about you.

This is the storyline of the book of Proverbs. Solomon is instructing his son to know the difference between two women: Harlot Folly and Lady Wisdom. The father wants his son to make friends with Lady Wisdom. He wants his son's life entangled with hers. In order to do that, he must learn to distinguish between the two women, in whatever forms they take: embrace the right and shun the wrong.

Harlot Folly and Lady Wisdom show themselves in the lives of people, male and female. Anywhere you meet someone who shuns the way of wisdom, you have met Harlot Folly. Anywhere you meet someone walking in the way of wisdom, you have met Lady Wisdom. What we are called to do is to befriend Lady Wisdom and shun Harlot Folly. Distinguishing between who will be your friend and who will not is a matter of life and death. Wisdom and folly are learned through friendship.

Friend

Our English word "friend" translates a number of different words in Scripture and can be used to characterize various relationships. The lover in the Song of Songs speaks of her beloved as her friend: "His mouth is most sweet, and he is altogether desirable. This is my beloved and this is my friend, O daughters of Jerusalem" (Song 5:16). A marriage can rightly be called a friendship.

Between the most intimate of relationships to the most superficial relationship, there is a spectrum of what counts as friendship. There may be an "intimate friend" (Prov 7:4), a "close friend" (Psa 41:9), a "familiar friend" (Psa 55:13), and more. The word "friend" can cover a wide range of relationships.

We may characterize this person as a friend and that person as an acquaintance. We also could distinguish friends by saying there is a difference between being friendly with many people and being friends.

The command to "love your neighbor as yourself" found in Leviticus 19:18 could also be translated "love your friend as yourself." The word translated "neighbor" is rightly translated "friend" elsewhere.

There are differing levels of intimacy in friendships, from the stranger on the street to a lifelong friend to a spouse. But we are all, to one degree or another, *entangled souls*. We are lives that are knit together. The stranger who is our friend is entangled with us because we are all human, descending from the same parents. His influence on us and our influence on him is not as immediate as a close friend, but we are still connected so that what each of us does affects the other.

Presently, I am speaking about those friends who are close to us, with whom we rub shoulders more often, those with whom we are more intimately connected. It is not merely an arrangement of some sort that simply puts two people in a similar context. Friendship is a connection of souls, our total animated lives joined to one another.

In many ways, deep friendship defies scientific definition. It is more poetry than prose. You two become more than the sum of the parts. There is a dynamic between you that cannot be fully explained.

Friends are not an optional feature in our life like whether or not to get the GPS or satellite radio feature on a new car. Friends are a necessity.

The Necessity of Friends

We are created in the image of a Triune God who is, to put it crudely, entangled within himself as Father, Son, and Spirit. Each person of the Trinity dwells within the other, a truth Jesus expresses in his prayer in John 17. Created in his image, we are relational beings, created by relationship, in relationship, and for relationship.

We are created by a relationship between a man and a woman which causes us to relate to the man and woman as father and mother. We share a common mission that cannot be completed by a single individual but through relationship. We need friendships, from the intimate "best friend" to a friendly society around us. To fulfill our purpose, we must have friends.

This is why it is foolish to try to isolate yourself. Proverbs 18:1 says, "Whoever isolates himself seeks his own desire; he breaks out against all sound judgment." Cutting yourself off from others, even if done with the excuse of being an introvert or being a schismatic jerk, is not a good thing.

Many times, Proverbs 18:1 is taken to refer to the hermit or, in our age, the introvert who does not really want to be around people. The principle may apply to him. He thinks that, for whatever reason, he does not need people. He can be like the Existentialist philosopher Jean-Paul Sartre who said, "hell is other people," keeping him from realizing his own existence and full potential because relationships got in the way. Such people, in the Christian world, are usually called "pietists." Some of these people believe they find personal holiness in their own private study and prayer time, cut off from relationships with the church or friends. In order to be holy, they need to be alone. This is just a form of what Proverbs warns against when it speaks of isolation.

Another possible meaning is suggested by Duane Garrett's translation of Proverbs 18:1: "A schismatic person seeks an opportunity for a quarrel; he rails against all sound policy."[1] This is the guy who always wants to be different, separating himself from others through his obnoxiously held opinions. He is always wanting to start something with others in order to distance himself from the crowd.

There are quite a few of these figures in the Reformed world in which I live. Such men believe they are showing

---

1. Garrett, 164.

themselves to be smarter than everyone else and that they really do not need anyone else. They are schismatic, entering conversations to disagree, being novel or disagreeable simply for the sake of being novel or disagreeable. Cutting yourself off from the larger body of the church or society through aggressive belligerence or through passive withdrawal is raging against all sound judgment and, therefore, not wisdom.

This does not mean you should go along to get along. Scripture is clear about this. The proverb means you should not cut yourself off from others because you do not think you need them. We cannot accomplish our mission apart from the imperfect church. Whatever the answer is, it is *not* to withdraw and isolate.

Because we were made in relationship and for relationships for the sake of fulfilling our purpose as the image of God, we need friendships. These friendships provide outside perspective in our lives and are created to be sources of wisdom. All wisdom does not reside in us as individuals, so we need the counsel of others from the time of birth to the time of death.

We are encouraged to seek counsel as a way of wisdom.

"Oil and perfume make the heart glad, and the sweetness of a friend comes from his earnest counsel" (Prov 27:9). Counsel from other people makes us glad because it protects us from making bad decisions.

"Without counsel plans fail, but with many advisers they succeed" (Prov 15:22).

"Where there is no guidance, a people falls, but
in an abundance of counselors there is safety"
(Prov 11:14; also 20:18; 24:6).

Whether they be government-level officials who are helping make decisions about war or a close friend who is helping you decide about a spouse, a friend's counsel is needed
because we do not know it all. We need someone or others
with different perspectives or more wisdom to come and
help us to see the things we cannot or will not.

All the proverbs concerning a multitude of counselors do not mean you need to have a huge committee of
friends helping you make decisions. The stress, rather, is on
the willingness of the individual to receive counsel. But if
you do not trust anyone, if you do not entangle your soul
with anyone, you are not putting yourself in a position to
receive counsel. Friendships must be established if you are
to have counselors because you must be able to trust your
counselor.

To have friends who will give you good counsel, you
cannot indiscriminately strike up relationships with everyone you meet. You need to be discriminate about those
friends who are closest to you.

The Need to Discriminate

"Discriminate" has become a dirty word in our society.
However, "to discriminate" simply means to distinguish by
making a judgment. People certainly discriminate based on
the wrong criteria, but there is nothing wrong with making

judgments. In fact, judgments are inevitable—even making judgments about those people who discriminate.

Solomon calls his son to be discriminatory with those he calls his closest friends. Why? What principle underlies the warnings in Proverbs about being choosey concerning your friends? Paul summarizes the intent with the proverbial statement, "Bad company corrupts good morals" (1 Cor 15:33). Paul is talking about associations with people who hold false beliefs about the resurrection, but the proverb is a general aphorism applied to a specific situation.

Your friends, the ones with whom you entangle your soul, shape you. We see this all the time and know it innately, but it is helpful to point it out and understand some of the reasons behind it. Psychologists and sociologists have written much, for example, about "crowd psychology" or even "mob mentality." When people get caught up in a movement with others or in a mob at a particular place, they tend to change, doing things they would not normally do as individuals. In a crowd, such people feed off of one another so as to embolden one another to keep pushing forward.

Think about the riots the US had in 2020. There was a spirit, an energy, that bound people together in which every scene escalated from small demonstrations to violence, looting, and burning. This happens frequently in our lives. When we open ourselves up to others, connecting with them emotionally, we allow them to dwell in us and we in them at some level. We begin to take up their mannerisms, whether in gestures or speech patterns. They do the same with us so that we are both becoming something different, growing together and changing as individuals.

This phenomenon is rooted in the Trinitarian relationships. As Father, Son, and Spirit dwell together intimately as one, each feeds off of the other, to put it crudely. They share life together. Each, though remaining individuals, eternally share the same attributes and character.

Created in God's image, our relationships change us. This can work for good or ill but it always works. The people to whom you open yourself up, the people with whom you entangle your soul, will change you. This can be anything from the music to which you listen to the people with whom you spend the most time.

Because of sin, we are drawn to disorder and rebellion. Remember, we have foolish hearts from childhood. This is why, as we will learn, we must make conscious decision to avoid entangling ourselves too much with wicked people. You become your closest associations. That is why you must be discriminatory in making and maintaining close friendships.

This is why Solomon instructs his son to choose the wise to be his friends while avoiding the foolish.

Choosing Friends Wisely

Before discussing the characteristics of the wise or foolish, remember that Proverbs is written by a father, imparting the instruction of a father and mother to a son.

Some want to flatten out the meaning of the recipient and say, "Anywhere you see 'son,' you can insert daughter as well." Not exactly. When Solomon instructs his son to avoid certain types of women, that is not just a metaphor, even though it can be extended to a metaphor. When Solomon tells his son to rejoice in the wife of his youth and to let her breasts satisfy him at all times, you cannot simply substitute the daughter for the son in that context without violating biblical law.

Proverbs is written to the son because the son is responsible for the mission. Proverbs is instruction for the son to find a helper who will help him with the responsibility God has given him. Much of what is said in Proverbs is geared toward male friendships: how to relate to other men and how a man ought to relate to a woman.

Proverbs does not treat friendships androgynously, as though males and females understand friendship in the same way. In fact, he recognizes they do not. But this does not mean ladies cannot learn about friendships from Proverbs, just as it would be wrong to say believers cannot learn from Paul's letters to pastors Timothy and Titus. Paul's letters were written to pastors, but the church learns from them in many ways, not only what pastors are supposed to be, but how members of a church can serve the Lord.

Thus, there are general principles that apply to both sexes. We learn, for instance, what character qualities a man should seek in a lady who is to be his wife, his close friend. From this principle, we learn how women ought to be developing their character to fulfill their God-given mission as a helper: Do not be like Harlot Folly. Be like Lady Wisdom.

Take another example. Proverbs 27:17 says that as iron sharpens iron, so a man sharpens the face of another. In general, this means good friends make you better so you can be productive. The image of iron sharpening iron and, specifically, saying that "one man sharpens the face of another" is directed toward men, probably indicating some of the characteristic roughness which men may have with one another. Men encourage one another through teasing or ragging one another. Women often do not understand this dynamic and consider it "mean" because, quite frankly, it is mean when women engage in such behavior. But guys sharpen one another through put downs as well as positive "atta boys." Women sharpen one another with tough words at times, but, generally, it is more through emotional connection.

The general principle in Proverbs 27:17, though, applies to both men and women. Proverbs is directed toward young men, so the images are more conducive to male relationships. However, young ladies may still learn about friendship in Proverbs, and how friends build up one another.

We are called to search out and form friendships with wise people. Throughout Proverbs, the son is called to make friends with Lady Wisdom. Friendship with her is integral to the son's mission.

Throughout the book she calls to him, and he is to search her out and heed her invitation. When he finds her and entangles his soul with her, she will do him good all the days of his life. At the conclusion of the book, we find that her husband is known in the gates when he sits among the elders (Prov 31:23). She has helped him rise into wise rule, kingship.

Lady Wisdom is symbolic, but she can be found in women. Young men need to seek out the companionship of a young lady who demonstrates the character of Lady Wisdom. Certainly, as a young lady she will not be mature in her wisdom, but she ought to be on the path. Young ladies should be cultivating the character of Lady Wisdom to prepare for this particular friendship just as men ought to be preparing themselves.

Proverbs 31 describes the character of Lady Wisdom as a lady who is trustworthy (vv. 11-12), industrious (vv. 13-19, 24, 27), benevolent (20), cares for her family (vv. 21, 27), adorns herself beautifully (v. 22), and is strong and honorable (v. 25). Young men, this is the lady you are seeking. Young ladies, this is the lady you must become.

We develop our character as men and women, not in isolation, but by the friendships we choose to have. Proverbs 13:20 says, "Whoever walks with the wise becomes wise, but the companion of fools will suffer harm." You must seek out friends who have their lives in proper order, who are faithful and fruitful.

Solomon tells his son the one who *walks with* the wise will be wise. You are to get on the path with him. When Jesus called his disciples, he told them to "follow me," not "go read these books" (though reading and listening would be involved). How much is learned, not by formal teaching, but by simply hanging around, observing, talking, and listening to wiser friends?

I remember just hanging around my grandpa while fishing, hunting, gardening, working on cars, mowing grass, and in other situations. I learned about life, what it was to be a man who takes care of his family and his property, how to relate to men and women, how to be productive with time, how to have fun and laugh, and when and how to show anger. I learned quite a few "redneck proverbs," which, according to my wife, are not all appropriate to share in public. That is okay. They were lessons for me along the way that I pass on to my children, though perhaps in modified form.

Wisdom with friends does not come through lectures but in living with one another, in walking together through life's decisions, learning how to deal with this and that in the situation. This is not to say you do not learn from books or lectures. This is not an either-or dilemma. But you cannot learn exclusively from books. In fact, Proverbs, along with the rest of Scripture, puts a premium on "walking with" the wise in order to learn wisdom.

In Deuteronomy 6, Moses instructed Israel to teach their children when you rise up, when you lie down, when you walk by the way. This is a way of life. The people with whom you *walk*, the people with whom you associate, they will teach you wisdom or folly. So, be careful with whom you walk.

In searching out friends, you want to find a faithful man. That quest is difficult at times, a truth that Solomon declares plainly in Proverbs 20:6: "Many a man proclaims his own steadfast love, but a faithful man who can find?" Solomon is not being cynical. He is acknowledging a real hardship. Good, faithful friends, those who have the character to swear to their own hurt as Psalm 15 says, who will stick by you even when it does not appear to be advantageous for them, those people are difficult to find. As the proverb says, many people may talk a good talk about their faithfulness, but who can find a man who has proven himself?

You also need to find a man who is willing to wound you when it is necessary. "Better is open rebuke than hidden love. Faithful are the wounds of a friend; profuse are the kisses of an enemy" (Prov 27:5-6). A person who is willing to tell you the truth about the wrong you are doing is a true friend. A person who is always sucking up to you, always avoiding subjects that might offend you, is your enemy. Friends encourage one another to holiness, and that requires being critical at times.

Our tendency is to despise the one who wounds us and love the one who flatters us. Who does not like to be "affirmed?" Why do you think all these deviants collect in groups? They all want to be affirmed or justified. Our tendency is to want to avoid pain, but these wounds from a person who genuinely loves us cleanse evil. "Blows that wound cleanse away evil; strokes make clean the innermost parts" (Prov 20:30). This, most likely, refers to corporal punishment, but it can also apply to psychological wounds as well.

This moves us right into how a good friend is like a sharpening tool: "Iron sharpens iron, and one man sharpens the face of a friend" (Prov 27:17). The imagery is intriguing and informative itself. The edge of a blade in Hebrew is sometimes called its "face." The face of a man is like a sword or axe. The imagery is not arbitrary. You and I need to be sharpened for the battle that comes with our dominion project, destroying enemies and clearing land to make it productive. An edge cannot be put on an iron blade with a cotton ball. You need something abrasive and as hard or harder than the iron itself to sharpen it. The person who corrects you is going to "wound" you, but you cannot get sharp without being wounded just as a blade cannot get sharp without peeling away the dullness through friction.

Sharpening one another does not mean always confronting what is wrong. Sharpening one another means encouraging and pushing the other when you are tempted to quit and sag. Having friends around you who condone and encourage mediocrity and sloth are bad for you. You need someone to push you, to make you ready for battle, whether with people or the non-human creation. As former Navy Seal Jocko Willink commonly says, "There is no growth in the comfort zone." Warriors do not get better with leaders who pacify them and coddle their softness. You do not get better by always taking the easy way. Good friends sharpen you by being hard on you like sharpening iron is to an iron blade. These are the types of friends you should pursue, but you must also actively avoid unwise friends.

And Harlot Folly, who is Lady Wisdom's antagonist, must be avoided like the plague. For young men she is easy on the eyes, appealing in her immediate availability, encouraging his sloth because he does not have to work for her at all. She is loud and loose, dressing like a whore (Prov 7:10-13), which means she wears clothes that say, "I'm sexually available right now." No patience is required to have her. She is a contentious woman, a nag, always bucking against leadership (Prov 19:13; 27:15; 21:9; 25:24). It is better to live in a corner of a housetop (21:19) or in a desert land (26:14-16) than to live with a quarrelsome wife. She may be physically attractive, catching your eye, but she has a devious, rebellious heart that will destroy your life, keeping you from fulfilling your mission because she is not interested in being a helper. She is the feminist, the career woman who scorns domestic duties (Prov 7:11) and motherhood. Young men, you do not want her as a friend-wife. She tears the house down instead of building it up.

Harlot Folly is not only seen in the female form, she is also expressed in any unwise and destructive friendships. Proverbs 1 describes a gang of young men which the son must avoid. They share characteristics with Harlot Folly. They are exciting and easy. You take what you did not work for. The gang appeals to young men because they demonstrate power. They are doing things and getting things done. They are cool and accomplishing things quickly, even though they are taking short-cuts.

Like Harlot Folly, the gang will eventually rob you of life. First appearances all look good, just as they do for a bird being baited into a net—free food! Everything is easy pickings. But the net ensnares you, and it is too late. You must be careful about getting caught up with cool trends and young men who try to take short cuts instead of putting in the work and living by God's law.

You must also avoid what we call "fair weather friends" as much as you are able. Proverbs 19:6-7 says, "Many entreat the favor of the nobility, And every man is a friend to one who gives gifts. All the brothers of the poor hate him; How much more do his friends go far from him! He may pursue them with words, yet they abandon him." If you begin to accomplish things in your life, your accomplishments will attract people who want to use you. In context, these proverbs speak about a judicial setting in which a rich man wields influence because people want what he has or do not want to get on his bad side because of what he can do to them. A poor man does not have that luxury. Anyone who sticks with the poor man even when it may be a disadvantage to him is a true friend. Sycophants do not make good friends.

Another type of person that Solomon warns his son to avoid is the *gossip*. "He who goes about as a talebearer reveals secrets; Therefore do not associate with one who flatters with his lips" (Prov 20:19). If a man is trying to destroy other men behind their backs, guess who's next? Friends like this can ruin your good name.

You are also to avoid *undisciplined* men. This lack of discipline shows itself in several ways. "Make no friendship with an angry man, And with a furious man do not go, Lest you learn his ways And set a snare for your soul" (Prov 22:24-25). There is nothing wrong with anger in itself as long as it is for the right reason and directed toward righteous ends. God is angry with the wicked every day (Psa 7:11). What is being said is that this man is characterized by anger. He cannot control it. It controls him.

Men especially like anger because it gives focus and feels powerful. That is why it is tempting. But focus also means you lose a broader perspective. Anger is needed at times to defeat evil, but if you are angry all the time, given to emotional outbursts and fits of rage, you lose all sense of proportion, act impetuously, always trying to gain control over people or a situation by force (whether psychologically or physically). The man who is angry all the time destroys those around him, ruining relationships, which is the opposite of wisdom's goal. Forging a friendship with a man given to anger will make you an angry man, and it will be a snare to your soul.

There are also the drunks and gluttons. "Hear, my son, and be wise; And guide your heart in the way. Do not mix with winebibbers, or with gluttonous eaters of meat; For the drunkard and the glutton will come to poverty, And drowsiness will clothe a man with rags" (Prov 23:19-21). Gluttons and drunkards only consume. They are not productive. Such behavior cannot go on forever, and you will wind up in poverty. You must discipline yourself in order to protect yourself from poverty.

Neither should you buddy-up with a thief. "Whoever is a partner with a thief hates his own life; He swears to tell the truth, but reveals nothing" (Prov 29:24). What happens here is that you become partners with a thief, learn what he is doing, but refuse to expose it. You may not be stealing, but you know that he is. But when you are partners or close friends with someone who does these things, even if you do not sin as he does, you will fall under the same curse. You are hurting yourself.

Of course, there are the super-spiritual Christians who think any kind of discrimination that weeds out unwise friends and only chooses wise friends is anti-Christian. They are all about grace and mercy. But if you become close friends with a person whose life trajectory is not on a wise path, you are not gracious. You are a fool according to Proverbs. You do not entangle yourself with someone who is in rebellion against God in order to "save them." You walk the path of wisdom with the wise and encourage them to join you. If they do not, you leave them behind.

Of the way of the wicked, Solomon says, "Do not enter the path of the wicked....Avoid it; do not go on it; turn away from it and pass on" (Prov 4:14, 15). This is what Jesus did. He cared for people. He called them like wisdom calls the simple in Proverbs. But he did not forsake the way of wisdom in order to befriend anyone. Either they joined him or he left them. He was even willing to do that with the twelve in John 6 and the crucifixion. If someone is not contributing to your walk as a godly person, as a better man or a better woman, you can be congenial, but you do not need to be close friends.

Your friendships are crucial in your learning wisdom. Choose wisely and choose the wise.

Proverbs 20:12

The hearing ear and the seeing eye,
Yahweh has made them both.

CHAPTER 9

Watch and Learn

Whenever you are trying to learn a skill, there is no substitute for seeing the skill in action. A man may spend a thousand hours in a flight school class, but if he has never been in the cockpit of an airplane with an experienced pilot, I really do not want to trust my life to him. The same could be said with a doctor, a carpenter, or a pastor. Developing vocational competency through apprenticeships is vital to any training. Students learn by observation from experienced men and women how to become skilled in a craft. There is no substitute for experience that comes through observing someone who is skilled in the area.

Wisdom, as we have been learning, comes from outside of us, ultimately through divine revelation but also through God's ordained means of parents and friends.

Combined with these is a power God has given to each of us that he expects to employ: observation.

Solomon tells his son, "The hearing ear and the seeing eye, Yahweh has made them both" (Prov 20:12). God has created us with sense perception. We can hear, see, smell, taste, and touch. Through our senses we interact with God and the world around us.

Worship, for example, has always engaged all the senses as God prescribes it in Scripture. God does not prescribe worship in a desolate space using only the ability to hear as the means of worship. He has an ornate tent constructed with details to see, with things to touch, bodily postures to assume, with odors to be smelled, as well as words and music to hear. Our relationship with God involves our whole person.

The way we relate to God in worship is also the way we relate to the world around us. We learn from interacting with the world through our senses. We taste so we can discern what is pleasant and what is foul. We touch in order to take hold of creation and change it. Our smell draws us to some things and repels us from others. We listen in order to learn. We look around us in order to distinguish between things.

The senses are not simply tools for survival, or pragmatic concessions without any spiritual purpose. We learn from Proverbs 20:12 that Yahweh has made both the hearing ear and the seeing eye. The eyes and ears may represent all senses, but Solomon is emphasizing these two, I think, for a reason. He is calling his son to use his God-given senses to figure out the way of wisdom in the world.

The ear is emphasized quite a bit through Proverbs: "Hear the instruction of your father" (Prov 1:8). But Yahweh has also made *the eye*. The eye is an instrument of judgment, observing, taking in things around us, and discerning. God has given us eyes, and he expects us to use them in our quest for wisdom. No, you cannot believe everything you see. Your vision is not an infallible judge of all things that come before your eyes. But your ability to observe things when governed by God's revelation should not be discounted.

Observation underlies many commands in Proverbs. For instance, when Solomon says, "Do not envy sinners," he assumes you are observing the lives of others and drawing conclusions (Prov 23:17-18; 24:1-2; 24:19-20). You *are* observing. You are using your eyes. God wants you to discipline them and use them to learn wisdom.

What are you looking for? Wisdom. Wisdom, remember, is understanding how relationships ought to work and the skill to make them do so. Wisdom is understanding how this thing or person over here relates to that thing or person over there in order to make the relationship good, true, beautiful, and productive. Wisdom is required for justice between people, putting people in right relationship with one another so that there can be a productive, joyful peace. Wisdom is required in working with inanimate objects in creating beautiful art. Bezalel, the craftsman that directed the construction of the Tabernacle, was filled with the Spirit of Wisdom for this purpose. Wisdom understands what good relationships are and skillfully puts all the pieces or people in those relationships.

You are looking for wisdom. How exactly do you find it through observation?

You discover wisdom through observing *patterns of relationships*. When you are looking at the world, you are looking at what types of behaviors have good results and what types of behavior have bad results.

I watch a man nailing boards together. I notice that every time he hits the nail directly on the head, the nail goes farther into the board and secures the joint. I also notice that every time he hits his thumb with the hammer, not only is the nail not going in the board, but he shakes his hand in pain and speaks in tongues. The right relationship is to avoid hitting my thumb and focus on the nail.

Simple, right? Yes. But there are actions that look immediately rewarding and good but have devastating long-term effects. The kind of observation to which we are called in Proverbs takes into account more than what is seen in the moment or even in a relatively brief period of time. The observations we are called to make are not short-sighted. Wise observation wants to know the long-term effects both in this life and the next.

I see that these people are having a great deal of fun in their drunkenness, gluttony, sexual promiscuity, and stealing. They are reaping immediate benefits from their actions. But what happens to people who live this way? What is the outcome of their lives in this life and the next?

If he is only looking for immediate gratification, the way of the fool is, many times, better than the way of the wise. The way of the wise is not immediately appealing because of its delayed gratification. Wisdom, many times, calls you to suffer now in order to enjoy reward later. Whether it is the diligent, persevering work of plowing, planting, and cultivating a garden or restraining your appetites, wisdom calls you to trust God for the long-term reward over the instant gratification.

When observing others and their actions, we keep the long game in mind and ask, "What does this action or habit look like in twenty-five to fifty years?" Solomon wants his son to work out the consequences of his choices so he can avoid destruction in the future and enjoy the life God created for him.

Also, your observation of human behavior cannot be *superficial.* Solomonic observation does not simply glance at something and make a judgment. Observation that yields insight requires pondering, meditating on what is going on. We live in an age where it is easy to manipulate one's image, whether because the press promotes certain personalities and denigrates others, or because social media allows people to project images of themselves and their families. It is easy to take superficial glances and draw conclusions quickly.

A hasty observation: "Man, I wish my family was as happy as theirs. What are we doing wrong?"

You need to understand that people who saturate social media with their "happy lives" are sometimes projecting wishes of what their lives could be. Sometimes it is real. Sometimes it is a phantasm. Superficial glances do not give you insight.

This is true in Hollywood and the church. Glamorous movie stars move through relationships quickly, rarely being satisfied. Christians on social media will present themselves as "living the dream." They appear to inhabit this great situation and their family is always happy. If you were to join them and live with them for a while, you would discover that it is not all they said it was.

Proverbs calls us beyond superficial observation. to learn the reality behind projected images. This is difficult because we live in a world of manipulated images, slogans and soundbites—all enemies of meditative observation. We are scrollers, and if it is not only a few words, we scroll right past it. If we cannot listen to it while we are doing something else, we certainly will not take the time to read it. Internet articles now publish expected read times: "Four-minute read."

In this age of scrolling, sloganeering, and soundbites, Proverbs calls us to patient meditation in our observation. Observe. Discover. What is really going on here? What are the consequences of these actions? What should my expectations be realistically?

You cannot engage in fruitful observation by isolating yourself either. It is not possible. We must observe the world through the fear of Yahweh, on the basis of divine revelation. These are the lenses through which you are observing the world, giving you insight as to *why* the patterns are the way that they are.

Wisdom begins with the fear of Yahweh (Prov 9:10), how he has revealed himself and our submission to him and love for him. He is the all-wise one. He knows how everything fits together. We need his revelation because we are creatures as well as sinners. God's revelation matures the vision of the creature and clears the vision of the sinner. Observing the world and making judgments apart from revelation only yields the frustrating search of Agur, the search that comes up empty until the seeker knows Yahweh. All observation needs a context, and our most fundamental context is the revelation God has given us through Christ Jesus and in his written word.

Remember, God's perspective is ultimate. He sees the end from the beginning. He knows the outcomes of all behaviors and decisions. Our observation needs to take on his perspective in order to see the world rightly and learn the way of wisdom.

Observing the Righteous

Proverbs calls us to seek out wise, righteous, godly examples in order to learn wisdom. In some ways, the call to observation is baked into all the language of being led by others or walking with others in the way of wisdom. For example, in Proverbs 4:11, Solomon tells his son he has "led him in the paths of uprightness." His son has walked with him, observing him all along the way. Observation is built into the way of discipleship. "Follow me" includes the call to "Imitate me."

The son is called to observe the skillful man in Proverbs 22:29: "Do you see a man skillful in his work? He will stand before kings; he will not stand before obscure men." You are to observe people who have been successful in their craft, find out what they did to get there, and follow that path. The skillful man put in time, effort, blood, sweat, and tears to get where he is. He has been patiently persevering, working when no one was looking. Now he stands before kings. He has a good reputation and is in demand for his work.

Do you want to be wise? Observe the wise and do what they do, adjusting for your situation.

In something of an ambiguous call, Solomon issues the exhortation, "My son, give me your heart, and *let your eyes observe my ways*. For a prostitute is a deep pit; an adulteress is a narrow well. She lies in wait like a robber and increases the traitors among mankind" (Prov 23:26-28).

There is much to be said about falling in with the wrong woman, but Solomon calls his son to let his eyes observe his ways. Solomon could be asking his son to heed his words, but it also may be that he is setting his life up as an example. The father is possibly the example of a life well-lived, avoiding harlot folly altogether. But we also know that Solomon had trouble with women who turned his heart from Yahweh (1 Kings 11:1-3). It also is a possibility that Solomon is telling his son, "I've had some experience in this area of sin. I've repented. Look at what happened to me and learn." Both are righteous examples, though the first is preferable.

Repentant people are righteous examples, some of whom have committed serious, life-altering sins. We learn from their righteousness in a life well-lived as well as from their repentance. Observing and imitating righteous examples is the way of wisdom, a theme not confined to Proverbs. Even though Jesus is much more than an example, he is the best example for us. When Peter is exhorting the scattered exiles, telling them to submit to authorities, he says, "For to this you have been called, because Christ also suffered for you, leaving you an example, so that you might follow in his steps" (1 Pet 2:21). In 1 Corinthians 4, Paul calls the Corinthian church to imitate him as children with a father. Hebrews 13:7 exhorts the church to look to the leaders as examples of how to live, considering the outcome of their way of life. Observing others' lives of righteousness is one of the means we have to learn how we ought to pattern our own lives. Our lives will not be exactly the same as our example. Paul was not calling the entire church in Corinth to become church-planting apostles. But there are patterns of wise behavior that can be applied to our lives.

There are some of us who have a greater responsibility to be examples. Parents, pastors, elders, mature men, and mature women ought to be examples to those younger. Older women, for instance, are to be reverent in behavior, not slanderers or slaves to much wine. As they live these righteous lives, they are to teach younger women to love their husbands and children, to be self-controlled, pure working at home, kind, and submissive to their own husbands, that the word of God be not blasphemed (Titus 2:3-5). Paul says they model these things in their lives, and it is through their lives that they teach the younger women. I am sure the young lady could learn in discussion, but the young lady must be able to see how this occurs.

As we are growing older and God places us in relationships, we have the light burden of living our lives in such a way that younger people can observe us and pattern their lives after us. This is one of the problems in the broader church. Men are being told to "man up" and women (if they corrected at all) are told to be "godly women," but given the general condition of our homes in this country and, quite frankly, in the church, they do not know what it means to "man up" or to be godly. We need parents, of course, teaching these things to their children by lifestyle.

But those who have not had such parents as examples might need mentorship so they can understand what it looks like to be a mature man or woman.

But there is also the burden on the disciple. You need to put yourself in a place to learn and put in the effort. The call in Proverbs is, in fact, primarily to the son who has the burden to discipline himself in humility to observe, learn, and imitate the wisdom of others.

The righteous are not the only ones we need to be observing.

Observing the Wicked

There are several sections in the book of Proverbs that share observations of the wicked. There is the scene with the foolish man and Harlot Folly in Proverbs 7:6-27. Solomon is looking out of his window, watching what transpires and learning from it. He observes how the young man puts himself in harm's way at night. He sees the craft of the woman who approaches him dressed as a whore. She is loud. She wants to be seen and desired by men in a cheap and easy way. She has her Only Fans page, wants to be friends on Facebook, puts her stuff up on TikTok and Instagram because she wants to draw the attention of young men. She is overly aggressive in a sexual manner, grabbing and kissing the young man, convincing him that she is a good Christian girl because she has been to worship.

What is Solomon doing? He is observing the tactics of Harlot Folly as well as the outcome for those young men who go to her, and he is learning: "You, my son, will just be the next victim. Don't think that you will be the one who will be different, who will save her or avoid destruction."

The same is true for the observation of the sluggard and his field in Proverbs 24:30-34. The speaker goes by the field of the sluggard, by the vineyard of a man lacking sense. He sees the results of the lack of diligence. The sluggard's vineyard is unfruitful and in disrepair. The speaker *looked* and *considered*, "How did it come to this?" Maybe the man fell ill and could not keep up his vineyard. But the speaker knows the situation and the man a little better obviously. The owner of the vineyard has been lazy, wanting to rest all the time when he ought to have been working. Now his garden is in disrepair and he is in poverty.

Watch and learn.

In other places Solomon tells us the punishment of the wicked is also instructive to the wise, who observe the consequences of sin and learn. "Strike the scoffer, and the simple will learn prudence..." (Prov 19:25; also 21:11). Observe others' mistakes and do not repeat them lest you fall under the same punishment. "Do you see a man hasty in his words? There is more hope for a fool than for him" (Prov 29:20). Observe what happens to a man who pops his mouth off all the time in a hasty fashion. The results are usually bad. Look at the fool: Observe the way he lives and the consequences, and adjust your life accordingly.

With this instruction, the question arises, "How do you observe the unrighteous and pass these judgments without becoming self-righteous?" Good question. There is always a danger of pride that will give birth to some form of self-righteousness.

Pride is believing you are completely self-made, that you rely on no one but yourself, and you refuse to give thanks to God for what you have. Sinful pride is a self-sufficiency and self-exaltation that refuses to acknowledge God's grace properly. Pride and its child, self-righteousness, are always waiting to pounce on us when we experience the blessings of following wisdom's way. However, distinguishing wisdom from foolishness is not self-righteousness.

Self-righteousness is trusting in oneself and one's own wisdom, not saying, "I'm doing what is right and he/she isn't." The Psalms are full of humble, righteous speech: I am not superior because of some self-generated wisdom but precisely because I am depending on what God says. Far from being self-righteous, I am being humble.

The fool is self-righteous because he has said, "No," to God and has chosen to establish his own form of righteousness. The fool's righteousness is based on wisdom divorced from God's revelation. As a faithful Christian, you must not let people play that game with you, flipping the script as if you are the one who is all uppity because things are working better for you or because you have lived according to God's wisdom. When they accuse you of self-righteousness, it is projection. They are accusing you of their own sin. Granted, no one who walks in wisdom should become arrogant, but again, arrogance is more of a self-reliance.

Guilt is a powerful weapon, and fools know how to use it to manipulate you to scorn your success and blessing because you followed God's wisdom. You are not self-righteous when you have worked diligently within God's boundaries and have become wealthy, skilled, fit, have a good marriage, or whatever so that now you are enjoying the benefits of the work and are confident. Many times it is envy that looks at you and calls you "self-righteous." Do not let the slothful, wicked fool define the terms, accepting his definitions. If you have gotten to where you are by doing things right, working hard, and treating people well along the way, do not accept the scorn of the "self-righteous," by those who are envious. Remain humble before God, acknowledging his grace, genuinely giving thanks, and keep doing what you are doing.

If we observe Wisdom's response to the recalcitrant fool, we will learn that, far from being cowed by some sort of guilt of self-righteousness, Wisdom is confident and mocks the fool when he reaps the consequences of his foolishness (Prov 1:24-27). You can be confident, not because you are relying upon your own wisdom, but because you are relying upon Wisdom himself.

Observing Non-human Creation

We are to observe the righteous and the wicked, but there is another part of creation we are called to observe.

There are a few times that Proverbs calls us to look at the creation around us and learn wisdom. Why can we learn wisdom from non-human creation? We learn in Proverbs 8 that Wisdom created everything, giving us a display of his glory. We see how God put things together, and we can follow his example.

We also can learn wisdom from non-human creation because all non-human creation symbolizes man in some way. We represent the height of God's creation as his image, his glory. We are made from the same stuff as animals, and so under the old covenant various animals could represent the worshiper before God. We spring from the ground like wheat so bread can represent our bodies. We are like trees called to bear fruit. We are like stars in the firmament. We have star dust, water, bug dust, grain dust, etc, all in us. God made them all, and they all reveal his glory. We are the apex of the revelation of his glory, and we share that feature with the rest of creation. The glory of the ant, rock badger, locust, and lizard are all revelations of God's glory, and they are revelations of us.

Consequently, Solomon tells his son to go to the ant in Proverbs 6:6, "Consider her ways and be wise." The ant does not suffer the fate of the sluggard because she is diligent about gathering food. Agur elaborates on this image in Proverbs 30 where he talks about not only the ant but the rock badger, locusts, and lizard. All these creatures seem to be extremely disadvantaged by size and strength, yet the ant provides for itself, the rock badger (coney) finds ways to protect itself, locusts have no king but cooperate as an army to wreak havoc, and the lizard, though small, lives in palaces. Kings learn how to carry themselves from observing the lion, the strutting rooster, and the he-goat (Prov 30:29-31).

These are given as examples, but they are not exhaustive. Learn from these, but also learn by the pattern which Proverbs lays down for you. Take time to observe creation. In Solomonic fashion, Jesus observes the creation and God's relationship to it and teaches his disciples about anxiety in Matthew 6. Look at the creation and learn wisdom.

Of course, it is in Christ Jesus himself that we see God's wisdom. Observe his life and its outcome. He entrusted himself to his Father, and the Father did not fail him. He delivered on all his promises. If one were in the situation and observing what was going on, seeing Jesus tortured and put to death without the perspective of God's word, you could become short-sighted. However, we have the benefit of seeing the outcome of walking wisdom's sometimes difficult path. The way of wisdom leads to life. We have seen it happen.

God has called you to observe, to discern wisdom from what you see all around you. Be disciplined to do so.

Proverbs 2:1-22

My son, if you receive my words
and treasure up my commandments with you,
making your ear attentive to wisdom
and inclining your heart to understanding;
yes, if you call out for insight
and raise your voice for understanding,
if you seek it like silver
and search for it as for hidden treasures,
then you will understand the fear of the LORD
and find the knowledge of God.
For Yahweh gives wisdom;
from his mouth come knowledge and understanding;
he stores up sound wisdom for the upright;
he is a shield to those who walk in integrity,
guarding the paths of justice
and watching over the way of his saints.
Then you will understand righteousness and justice
and equity, every good path;
for wisdom will come into your heart,
and knowledge will be pleasant to your soul;
discretion will watch over you,
understanding will guard you,
delivering you from the way of evil,
from men of perverted speech,
who forsake the paths of uprightness

to walk in the ways of darkness,
who rejoice in doing evil
  and delight in the perverseness of evil,
men whose paths are crooked,
  and who are devious in their ways.
So you will be delivered from the forbidden woman,
  from the adulteress with her smooth words,
who forsakes the companion of her youth
  and forgets the covenant of her God;
for her house sinks down to death,
  and her paths to the departed;
none who go to her come back,
  nor do they regain the paths of life.
So you will walk in the way of the good
  and keep to the paths of the righteous.
For the upright will inhabit the land,
  and those with integrity will remain in it,
but the wicked will be cut off from the land,
  and the treacherous will be rooted out of it.

CHAPTER 10

The Pursuit of Wisdom

In America, we have developed more and more into a service economy. We still produce goods, but over the past few decades, we have outsourced a great deal of manufacturing to foreign countries. We need service industries as a part of our economy to be sure. Where would we be without doctors, lawyers, lawn services, utilities, restaurants, and other services? Service industries, like the rest of the economy, are driven by consumers' desires, and the businesses that meet those desires the fastest fare the best. Chick-Fil-A can get you through the drive-thru in ninety seconds with a decent bag of food. You can order from Amazon with a few swipes on your phone and, in some places, have it delivered by drone or courier within a few hours. Expectations rise for the consumers. To stay competitive, companies have to make it easier and faster to get products.

There is nothing inherently wrong with this, but it may start to shape the way we think and interact with the world. We want things fast and easy because companies want to please us as consumers. We can be easily frustrated if a store does not have a product or we cannot get something we want within a day or two.

In the midst of this ever-increasing speed by which we acquire everything is the call to patiently pursue wisdom, a life-long journey. There is nothing fast-and-easy about it. But if we are going to be wise, we must not allow ourselves to get caught up in this fast-and-easy mentality and learn patient pursuit.

Wisdom is something that must be learned, and it is learned by pursuit; that is, you have to be aggressive to learn it. The need to pursue wisdom at some stage of life assumes that we are called to pursue wisdom. Solomon makes it clear the pursuit of wisdom is, indeed, our calling.

In Proverbs 3:13, we are told that the man is blessed who *finds* wisdom, which assumes he has searched for it. Proverbs 4 encourages the son to "get wisdom" (4:5, 7) and that wise words are life to all those who *find* them (4:20-21). Wisdom calls the young man to pursue her in Proverbs 8:1-11 and in 9:1-6. In Proverbs 23:12, the young man is encouraged to *apply* his heart to instruction, to give himself over to hearing it. In Proverbs 24:13-14, wisdom is compared to the drippings of the honeycomb and is a blessing when it is found.

We hear the call most clearly in Proverbs 2, where Solomon tells his son about the benefits of treasuring up his commandments, making his ear attentive to wisdom, inclining his heart to understanding. The son should call out for insight and raise his voice for understanding. He is to seek it as silver and search for it as hidden treasure.

Wisdom is to be sought after, pursued diligently. However, we only pursue wisdom because Wisdom first pursues us. The exhortations in Proverbs 2 follow the revelation of Wisdom in Proverbs 1. We read beginning in Proverbs 1:20 that Wisdom cries aloud in the street, raises her voice in the markets. A similar call is found in Proverbs 8:1ff. Wisdom calls. Wisdom pursues us.

How does wisdom pursue us, calling out, raising her voice? Wherever God has made himself known, Wisdom is calling. We read in Psalm 19 that God does this wordlessly through the created order as well as through the words of Scripture. Because of sin, we cannot understand the wisdom of the created order as we should without the revelation of Scripture, nevertheless, Wisdom is thunderously calling all around us. Paul is clear about this in Romans 1 when he says:

> For the wrath of God is revealed from heaven against all ungodliness and unrighteousness of men, who by their unrighteousness suppress the truth. ***For what can be known about God is plain to them, because God has shown it to them.*** For his invisible attributes, namely, his eternal power and divine nature, have been ***clearly perceived***, ever since the creation of the world, ***in the things that have been made.*** So they are without excuse. For although they knew God,

> they did not honor him as God or give thanks to him, but they became futile in their thinking, and their foolish hearts were darkened. ***Claiming to be wise, they became fools***, and exchanged the glory of the immortal God for images resembling mortal man and birds and animals and creeping things (Rom 1:18-23)

Men *suppress* the truth in unrighteousness, but they are suppressing it, not completely ignorant of it. They exchange God's wisdom for their own and become fools.

Wisdom's voice is raised, calling out wordlessly in the creation. Wisdom's voice is raised, calling out verbally through the proclamation of the gospel, the instruction of parents, friends, and other sages. The pursuit, as is clear in Proverbs, is intended to bring people into its way of life, not merely suggestive echoes of an optional but unnecessary way of life. Wisdom's call is a royal call, a summons from the throne, that chases down the inhabitants of the earth, calling them to loving allegiance to their God and king.

Wisdom expects your response. There is an interesting connection between Wisdom's call in Proverbs 1:20 and what Solomon exhorts his son to do in Proverbs 2:3. Wisdom pursues the simple, "raising" her voice in Proverbs 1:20. In Proverbs 2:3, Solomon's son must "raise" his voice in pursuit of Wisdom. The same verb is used in both verses. Just as Wisdom pursues you, you are to pursue Wisdom.

Because you know your response is a response to pursuing Wisdom, you are assured that Wisdom is not teasing you, suggesting promises on which she will never deliver.

Wisdom wants to be found. When you pursue her as she wants to be pursued, she is ready to be found. She will be found, and this is an assurance that Solomon makes clear beginning in Proverbs 2:5: "...*then* you will understand the fear of Yahweh and find the knowledge of God. For Yahweh gives wisdom."

This is the promise we hear in James 1:5-8, when praying for wisdom during times of tribulation so you may know how to endure faithfully, but the promise that God will grant wisdom relies on a deeper principle and promise in Scripture found in Proverbs: Ask for wisdom, seek wisdom, call out and raise your voice for wisdom, and you will find her.

Pursuing Wisdom assumes several realities. First, *you do not have wisdom.* You do not pursue something you already have. You pursue that which you do not have. The command to pursue wisdom assumes you do not have wisdom. Solomon affirms elsewhere that foolishness is bound up in our hearts from birth. Foolishness is not intellectual disability but a moral deficiency, a rebellion against God. Though foolishness is driven from our hearts through the rod and instruction when we are young and through self-discipline and purposeful, determined pursuit of wisdom as we age, we will never be all-wise, so there will always be a lack and, therefore, a reason to pursue wisdom.

Second, the call to pursue Wisdom assumes that *wisdom is outside of you.* We know from Proverbs 2:6 that only Yahweh gives wisdom. Wisdom comes from him and not from within ourselves. But it is not as though we depend upon God directly without any mediation, as though we sit on a mountain top or in the privacy of our prayer closets and receive wisdom like a data download from God. As we have learned, there is a premium in Proverbs on learning wisdom from parents, friends, and other wise people. We depend on relationships with others to learn wisdom, especially from those older than us. Pursuing wisdom assumes I cannot rely upon myself but must rely upon God and those wise people he has put all around me.

A third assumption about the pursuit of wisdom is that *wisdom is, to one degree or another, hidden.* Even though Wisdom pursues, calling to all of us, getting to know Wisdom is not easy. There are mysteries to Lady Wisdom that must be discovered. This hiddenness of wisdom is hinted at when Solomon tells his son he must search for Wisdom as for hidden treasure. Proverbs 25:2 makes this plain when we are told, "It is the glory of God to conceal a matter, it is the glory of kings to search a matter out." Wisdom does not tease. She will deliver on her promises. But you must seek her. Her beauty is not merely skin deep. While she is attractive, adorning herself beautifully (Prov 31:17, 25), she also adorns the hidden person of the heart as Peter speaks about in 1 Peter 3:4. You only discover the richness and depth of her beauty when you pursue her so you may know her.

The fourth assumption about the pursuit of wisdom is that *wisdom requires work in thinking and acting.* Pursuing wisdom requires, listening, meditative reflection, *and* action. Solomon tells his son how to pursue wisdom in the first sections of Proverbs 2.

In poetic parallel statements in Proverbs 2:1–2, Solomon focuses on *the ear,* receiving his words and making the ear attentive to wisdom. In order to pursue wisdom, you must be an active listener. This requires a humility that recognizes the truth that you are not all-wise and never will be, that wisdom comes from outside of you. Listening is an act of submission. God calls you to *hear* or *listen to* his word, seeking to understand what is said. Listening is not thinking about what you are going to say next or catching bits and pieces of what is said with preconceived ideas to shape the other's words into what you want them to be. Listening is taking to heart what the other person is actually saying. Wherever wisdom calls, we are to listen.

We must listen to the instruction given by wise parents, friends, pastor, elders, and others who are speaking to us. But pursuing wisdom goes beyond listening, at times being a captive audience. Pursuing wisdom means chasing down wisdom and putting yourself in a place to listen, actively reading books, listening to good podcasts, and a multitude of other media.

We pursue wisdom not only by listening but also by *treasuring up* wise commandments and inclining our hearts to understanding (Prov 2:1, 2). What you treasure is that which is of greatest value to you. Jesus said that where a man's treasure is there will his heart be also (Matt 6:21; Luke 12:34).What you value most will be evident in what you pursue and guard. Solomon tells his son wisdom ought to be treasured.

But treasuring up also implies that wisdom is being stored up for a purpose down the road. There are some words of wisdom that are not immediately applicable. Some words of wisdom may not seem immediately useful, and foolish people ignore them or pass them off: "Whatever." If it is not a step-by-step instruction manual or You-

Tube video for what I may be facing at this moment, I do not want to hear it. That is the attitude of a fool.

Wisdom involves learning *perspective*. Without proper perspective, without a larger worldview to interpret all those step-by-step instructions, you are tossed about by every new fad. You have no foundation. The Scriptures reveal wisdom, not just in straightforward commands and proverbs, but also in the details of the laws concerning offerings, leprosy, the elements of the Tabernacle, the reason Israel did not eat the meat of the hip joint, and many other things that do not seem immediately useful to us.

When practicality is not immediately apparent—if we cannot walk out with a "to do list"—we may tend to think that Bible teaching is irrelevant: "I need to know how to hack it on Monday." Certainly, Bible teachers need to demonstrate how your life fits into God's story for Monday morning, but there also needs to be some patience.

For instance, learning about the construction of the Tabernacle or Temple does not seem immediately applicable. We read through the last chapters of Exodus, and it is all about curtains, boards, furniture, utensils, and more, with an interesting story about the golden calf stuck in the middle. The end of Ezekiel is all about the dimensions of the new Temple, and it all seems to drone on and on. Our eyes glaze over and our ears begin to shut out the sound. We do not like these things because we do not understand them, and, many times, we do not understand them because we do not have the patience to learn about them. But all the construction details shape the way you think about yourself, the church, the universe and how all of it relates to God. This perspective helps the commandments of God make sense because they make sense of what he is doing and our mission in the world. We do not think studying something like this is practical or relevant, but it is the revealed wisdom of God, and if we meditate upon it, work at it, and treasure it up in our hearts, God's wisdom becomes evident.

Take, for instance, God's purpose in revealing the structure of the Restoration Temple through Ezekiel to Israel:

> As for you, son of man, describe to the house of Israel the temple, *that they may be ashamed of their iniquities*; and they shall measure the plan. And if they are ashamed of all that they have done, make known to them the design of the temple, its arrangement, its exits and its entrances, that is, its whole design; and make known to them as well all its statutes and its whole design and all its laws, and write it down in their sight, *so that they may observe all its laws and all its statutes and carry them out. This is the law of the temple*: the whole territory on the top of the mountain all around shall be most holy. Behold, *this is the law of the temple* (Ezek 43:10-12).

The structure of the temple *is* the law, the commandments. The structure of the Temple reveals iniquities.

Learning about God striking the hip of Jacob and how Israel did not eat the hip portion of meat, or why we care about lizards making clay pots unclean, or why a potter's field was bought by the Temple officials with the betrayal money of Jesus does not tell you how to fix your car or rear your children. But meditating on the Scriptures, immersing yourself in the story, treasuring the revealed wisdom of God will help you in the long run as you seek to put things in the world into right relationships in the execution of your dominion mission.

Do not dismiss words of wisdom that are not immediately relevant to your situation. Pursuing wisdom means treasuring things up in your heart, holding on to them as things of great value because one day they will help you make sense of life and how to fulfill you mission.

In the pursuit of Wisdom, Solomon also calls his son to *prayer*, calling out for insight, raising his voice for understanding (Prov 2:3). Prayer is a recognition of dependence, that you are not self-sufficient, that wisdom does not reside with you but comes from Yahweh (Prov 2:6). But prayer should not be thought of as, say, the ancient world thought of asking things from their gods. Their gods were distant; there was basically a commercial relationship between them, a highly impersonal exchange of goods. Christian prayer, on the other hand, is being caught up into the life of God himself, fellowshipping with him.

Praying and asking for wisdom, therefore, is not about God dropping some wisdom package from the sky, a thing to be received like an Amazon package from a heavenly drone. Wisdom is raising her voice (Prov 1:20; Prov 8:1), and you are raising your voice in answer. There is a dialogue. God grants wisdom through prayer, but he does so within this vital relationship, as he interacts with you in worship, through parents, friends, and family members in Christ. Wisdom is found in a vital, active, dialogical relationship with God. As you live in right relationship with him, worshiping, praying faithfully, you gain wisdom.

Solomon also tells his son directly that pursuing wisdom involves *seeking it like silver and searching for it as hidden treasures.* Seeking and searching for silver and hidden treasures speaks to the desire, drive, and diligence you have when you know something of great value can be found and possessed.

Imagine if someone told you the house you bought was the house of a very rich man who did not trust the banks or stock market but kept all his wealth in gold. He suddenly died in that house. It was discovered in a document after you bought the house that he had hidden all his gold in a secret place in the house, not bequeathing it to anyone and having never given it away. You know that somewhere in the house there is a stockpile of gold bullion.

Maybe, because you are so super spiritual, you would say, "Who cares," and not search for the gold. I, however, would not sleep until I found the gold. (Obviously, Solomon does not think it beneath spirituality to search for valuable treasures. That's why he made the comparison.) This is the diligence expected of someone searching for wisdom.

We have learned *where* you search for wisdom—principally in the Scriptures, through parents, friends, and other wise people—but *how* you search for wisdom, diligently searching with perseverance, driven by what you believe is valuable. Seeking and searching is *action*. While contemplative meditation is necessary in the pursuit of wisdom, doing things is also necessary.

I am sure that when Adam began farming, even though God had demonstrated many things to him in planting the Garden, there were still many things to learn. "How does this fit with that and what can I use to accomplish the purpose?" It was during such moments that WD-40 and duct tape were discovered. If it moves and it should not, use duct tape. If it does not move and it should, use WD-40. Adam acted in the world, and through trial-and-error he learned how things worked and what tools he needed to get them to work. We learn wisdom through acting, not without thinking first, but our thinking in itself is not sufficient.

When my second son was in high school, he was part of a robotics team called "Engineers of Tomorrow." Because he was involved, I was involved. We had seasoned engineers and college students. The college students had all the new tech and all the formulas they learned in class. They would draw up things on the computer and think that it would work. The seasoned engineers would say, "Draw it up on the dry erase board, build a prototype, see if it works, adjust it, and then, when you know what works, draw it up on the computer program." Spending hours and hours drawing things up on the computer without putting your hands to the project generally did not work out well. It all made perfect sense, but there was one problem: it did not work. Reality does not always line up with theories. You have to try things out to learn if they work.

This searching implies that *patience* is involved as well as diligence. Sometimes we can become extremely excited about the pursuit of something and hit it hard and fast. But when we do not see immediate results, we become discouraged and give up. "I ate a salad for lunch. Why haven't I dropped five pounds today?!" You must be patient, trusting the promises of God about the pursuit of wisdom. You cannot learn to be a doctor or an engineer in a day or a week. What makes you think you can learn wisdom any faster? Seek diligently, but seek patiently. *Festina Lente*: "make haste slowly," an old Greek adage (translated into Latin) that was a favorite of Augustus Caesar. The adage conveys the spirit of diligence that Solomon is exhorting. Do not be rash. Be bold. Pursue. But do so with thoughtfulness.

We are to pursue wisdom, but when should we do it? Is there an optimal time? Yes, there is. Wisdom is to be pursued when you are *young*. When you are a child, parents are the primary pursuers of wisdom on your behalf, correcting you with the rod and instruction. But the fact that parents are commanded and exhorted to drive foolishness from the hearts of children means the pursuit of wisdom begins at birth. It is not something to be delayed until a later age. Jesus grew in wisdom from the time he was a small child (Luke 2:40, 52). In doing so, he gave a pattern for all children to follow.

In the broader church, we have come to expect a pattern with our children. I watched it over and over again growing up and even now that I am older. Here is the typical pattern: Be converted and baptized, grow into your mid to late teens and sow your wild oats through college, then settle down, get married, have children, get back in church, and start the process all over again. This pattern is practically accepted as axiomatic in the broader Christian world. This is just the way things are. But this is not the pattern of wisdom; this is not the pattern parents should expect of their children.

Parents, we should expect our children to pursue wisdom from their earliest ages with us providing examples and instruction in how to do it.

Children, you have responsibility to pursue wisdom just as your parents have the responsibility to teach you wisdom. You do not get to flirt with Harlot Folly because you are young and will have plenty of time for all that wisdom stuff later. You have responsibilities before God right now to obey him, and that obedience involves giving yourself to the pursuit of wisdom under the guidance principally of your parents.

Parents, expect it and teach it. Children, listen and learn.

You are to pursue wisdom when you are young, but you also must pursue wisdom when you are old. Proverbs is written to give prudence to the simple, knowledge and discretion to the youth, but the wise also must hear and increase in learning (Prov 1:4, 5). Because we will never be all-wise, there will always be room to learn wisdom.

You are to pursue wisdom when you young, when you are old, and *right now*. Obedience to wisdom's call should not be delayed. So, maybe you have not walked in wisdom up to this point. You think there is nothing that you can do since you did not start pursuing wisdom when you were young. That is not true. Start at whatever stage of life you are in. Yes, there are people who are way ahead of you. Yes, you may face consequences from a life not lived by wisdom. No, the end of folly does not have to be your fate. If you hear wisdom's call (and you are hearing it now), now is the time to pursue wisdom. All those people around you who are beyond you should not intimidate you. Do not let pride stand in the way of learning wisdom. If you have many wise people surrounding you in the church, this simply means you have a wealth of resources.

You learn wisdom when you are young, when you are old, and *continuously*. The learning of wisdom should not be a matter of fits and starts but a continuous journey. It is a way that is walked. You learn wisdom by getting up in the day that God gives you and pursuing it that day. You do that day after day. No secret silver bullets, just steady persevering, disciplined pursuit.

So, brothers and sisters, young and old, pursue wisdom. If you do not pursue wisdom, you will never know wisdom.

www.ingramcontent.com/pod-product-compliance
Lightning Source LLC
Chambersburg PA
CBHW071325120626
46546CB00002B/442